Growing with Music

HARRY R. WILSON

WALTER EHRET

ALICE M. SNYDER

EDWARD J. HERMANN

ALBERT A. RENNA

Illustrated by JOHN MOODIE

BOOK 3

Prentice-Hall, Inc.
Englewood Cliffs, New Jersey

The authors of GROWING WITH MUSIC wish to thank the many people who have contributed original material for this book. Every effort has been made to locate owners of other materials and grateful acknowledgment is due these publishers for permission to reprint copyrighted materials. The authors also wish to thank the Prentice-Hall Music Department editorial staff—Wallace W. Schmidt, John G. Detroy, Harry G. Trebilcox, Madeleine A. Dufay, and Mary G. Whitcomb—for their invaluable assistance and many original contributions to the GROWING WITH MUSIC series.

HARRY R. WILSON, *Chairman of the Music Department*
Teachers College, Columbia University

WALTER EHRET, *Supervisor of Vocal Music*
Scarsdale Schools, Scarsdale, New York

ALICE M. SNYDER, *Professor of Music Education*
San Francisco State College

EDWARD J. HERMANN, *Associate Professor of Music*
Louisiana State University

ALBERT A. RENNA, *Director of Music*
San Francisco Unified School District

As an aid to teaching and interpretation, all songs in "Growing with Music,"
Book 3, are recorded and are available in a boxed set
of 12-inch L.P. records, from Prentice-Hall, Inc.

The music in this book was reproduced from handwritten originals by Maxwell Weaner.

Printed in the United States of America

36610-E

Contents

Old folks, young folks,
Children always gay;
Boys and girls a-growing
While singing at their play.
—ANONYMOUS

MOOD IN MUSIC

We're All Together Again

TRADITIONAL

Gaily

We're all   to-geth-er a - gain, We're here, we're here! __

We're all   to-geth-er a - gain, We're here, we're here!

Glad   to   be   sing - ing all   to - geth-er a - gain,

Sing - ing all   to-geth-er a - gain, We're here, we're here! __

1

Good Friends

WORDS BY M. V. BANNON
NORWEGIAN FOLK TUNE

Is the mood of this song the same as the song on page 1? How are they different? Both songs are about friends.

Steadily

Good friends go hand in hand And al - ways un - der-stand

Friend - ship be - gins with two, Loy - al and true.

So when we meet or part, It's with an o - pen heart.

I give my hand to you, Old friends and new!

2

Just Wishing

WORDS BY MADELEINE A. DUFAY
MUSIC BY GRANT BEGLARIAN

Wistfully

1. Wish it were sun - ny, gold - en as hon - ey,
2. Wish there were show - ers, go - ing for hours, ___

Down where the riv - er is run - ny. I'm wish - ing,
Sprin - kling on me and the flow - ers. I'm wish - ing,

just wish - ing, A min - now I could be fish - ing.
just wish - ing, A pud - dle I could be squish - ing.

3. Wish it were snowing,
   Then I'd be going,
   Finding the best snow
       for throwing.
   I'm wishing, just wishing,
   A snowball I could be
       pitching.

3

In Father's Flower Garden

WORDS BY ADELE ST. ETIENNE
FRENCH FOLK MELODY

Happily

1. In fa - ther's flow - er gar - den,
2. The birds are gai - ly fly - ing

the li - lacs you will see, ___
and sing - ing mer - ri - ly, ___

The birds are gai - ly fly - ing
The quail, the pret - ty par - tridge,

and sing - ing mer - ri - ly.
the rob - in in the tree.

3. The quail, the pretty partridge,
   the robin in the tree
   Will never leave the garden,
   they sing for you and me.

4

Refrain

Ah, near to my fair one, it's so good to be, to be,

Ah, near to my fair one, it's so good to be. ___

In the last four measures of
this song, the melody uses
only the tones of the I chord.

Sweep, Sweep Away

WORDS BY W. S. HAYNIE
CREOLE FOLK SONG

Softly

Sweep, sweep, sweep a - way,   Sweep the road of dreams,

Peo - ple say   that, in the night, 1. The tur - tle will
2. The croc - o - dile

talk, it   seems.   The tur - tle will   talk   it   seems.
weeps big   tears.   The croc - o - dile weeps big   tears.

5

Cotton-Eye Joe

TENNESSEE LULLABY

Wistfully

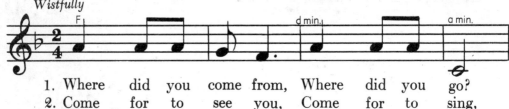

1. Where did you come from, Where did you go?
2. Come for to see you, Come for to sing,

Where did you come from? ⅞ Cot - ton - Eye __ Joe?
Come for to show you My dia - mond __ ring.

3. Where did you get it? How did it grow?
   Who could've made it, Cotton-Eye Joe?

4. Comes from the mine fields, Comes from the ground,
   Comes from the darkness, With night all around.

5. Why does it sparkle? What makes it glow?
   Why is it gleaming, Cotton-Eye Joe?

6. Light makes it glitter, Sun from the skies,
   Wants to be shinin', Like your bright eyes.

From "American Ballads and Folk Songs," © 1934 by John and Alan Lomax.
© assigned 1958 to Ludlow Music, Inc., New York, N. Y. Used by permission.

Hush-a-by

AMERICAN FOLK SONG

Softly

Hush - a - by, don't you cry,

Go to sleep, my lit - tle ba - by. *Fine*

When you wake, you shall have

All the pret - ty lit - tle po - nies.

Blacks and bays, dap - ples and grays,

D. C. al Fine

All the pret - ty lit - tle po - nies.

I Want to be Ready

SPIRITUAL

How many repeated
phrases can you
find in the second
part of this song?

Steadily

I want ___ to be read - y,

I want ___ to be read - y, ___

I want ___ to be read - y ___

To walk in Je - ru - sa - lem, just like John.

Solo ad lib

1. John said the cit - y was just four - square,
2. Oh, John! Oh, John! What do you say?

Group

Walk in Je - ru - sa - lem, just like John.

And he de - clared he would meet me there,
That I'll be there at the com - ing day.

Walk in Je - ru - sa - lem, just like John.

Seven Stars A-Shining

WORDS AND MUSIC
BY JOAN HAINES

Can you make up other verses
to fit the mood of the song?

Slowly

1. Sev - en stars a - shin - ing,

Shin - ing on my ba - by in the nest,

Oh, my dar - ling, Close your eyes, the world's going to rest.

2. Seven ships a-sailing,
   Sailing to my baby in the nest,
   Oh, my darling, Close your eyes,
   the world's going to rest.

3. Seven dreams a-drifting,
   Drifting to my baby in the nest,
   Oh, my darling, Close your eyes,
   the world's going to rest.

9

Child's Evensong

WORDS AND MUSIC
BY JOHN STAINER

God's lark at morning I would be!
I'd set my heart within a tree
Close to His bed and sing to Him
Right merrily
A sunrise hymn.
—WILLIAM ALEXANDER PERCY

Andante

1. From the heav'n a - bove us, 'Mid the an - gels mild,
2. Boun-teous-ly He gives us Food and rai - ment still,

Looks a lov - ing Fa - ther Down on ev - 'ry child.
Gra-cious-ly He keeps us From each threat-'ning ill.

Ten - der - ly He lis - tens When He hears us pray,
Praise the lov - ing Fa - ther, Of His good - ness tell;

Faith - ful - ly He guides us On our earth - ly way.
He will not for - sake us, He doth love us well.

Here is one rhythm pattern that you will find in this melody:

What other pattern can you find? Each line of the song is one phrase.
How many patterns are there in each phrase?

10

Dream Song

What words would you use
to tell a friend about
the mood of this song?

WORDS BY EDWINA WELLS
RUSSIAN FOLK TUNE

Peacefully

1. Foun-tains flow-ing, moon-light glow-ing,
2. Rain-drops fall-ing, crick-ets call-ing,

White sails   on   the   sea,
Brook-lets   run - ning   free,

Wild birds fly - ing, sun-sets dy - ing,
Pine   trees sigh-ing, winds re - ply-ing,

Bring   a   dream to   me. ____
Sing   a   song   to   me. ____

With My Wooden Shoes

WORDS BY MADELEINE A. DUFAY
FRENCH FOLK TUNE

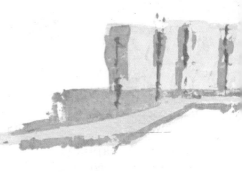

Briskly

Refrain

Through Lor - raine I went a - walk - ing
En pas - sant par la Lor - rai - ne

With my wood - en shoes, ____
A - vec mes sa - bots, ____

1. Heard three cap - tains gai - ly clap - ping,

With my wood - en shoes a - tap - ping,

Oh, oh, oh! With my wood - en shoes. __
A - vec mes sa - bots. __

12

2. When the captains
heard me coming,
On their drums they
started drumming.

3. Oh, I heard the
captains talking
In Lorraine when
I went walking.

Funeral March of a Marionette

BY CHARLES FRANCOIS GOUNOD

Charles Gounod is best remembered as the composer of several very serious operas and oratorios. His most famous composition is the opera "Faust."

However, not everything Gounod wrote was serious. His humor can be heard in this piece. We usually think of funerals as very solemn occasions, but this is the funeral march of a puppet. You can tell from this perky little tune that the march should not be taken too seriously or sadly.

Can you name the instrument that plays the melody?

Sky Music

WORDS AND MUSIC
BY JOAN HAINES

Slowly

Who can sing —— the song the wind is sing-ing? ——

Who can hear —— his mu - sic in the sky?

Ooh, _____ Ooh, _____

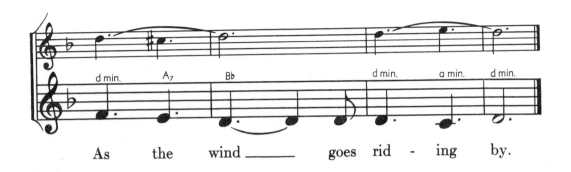

As   the   wind _____ goes rid - ing   by.

Day's End

This is a calm song.
How will the mood change
if you sing it much faster?

WORDS BY YVONNE CARR
MUSIC BY H. G. NAGELI

Moderately

When the day is end - ing, pur - ple twi - light falls,

O - ver dark-ened hills the lone-ly whip-poor-will calls.

2. Now the sun is painting,
with a palette bold,
Slowly drifting clouds
in brilliant crimson
and gold.

Goodbye Ol' Paint

TRADITIONAL COWBOY SONG

Moderately

Refrain

Good - bye, ol' Paint, I'm a - leav - in' Chey - enne,

Good - bye, ol' Paint, I'm a - leav - in' Chey - enne.

Verse

1. My foot in the stir - rup, my po - ny won't stan', —
2. I'm a - rid - in' ol' Paint an' a - lead - in' ol' Dan, —
3. My foot in the stir - rup, my bri - dle in han', —

I'm a - leav - in' Chey - enne an' I'm off for Mon - tan'. —
Good - bye, lit - tle An - nie, I'm off for Mon - tan'. —
I'm a - leav - in' Chey - enne an' I'm off for Mon - tan' —

16

RHYTHM AND DANCE

Dance of Greeting

WORDS BY E. J. HERMANN
DANISH FOLK TUNE

Happily

Bow to your part - ner, Bow to your neigh - bor,

Stamp! Stamp! And turn your - self a - round.

1. Join hands and cir - cle left, ___ Cir - cle left to - geth - er,
2. Join hands and cir - cle right, ___ Cir - cle right to - geth - er,

Join hands and cir - cle left, To - geth - er here we go.
Join hands and cir - cle right, To - geth - er here we go.

3. Join hands, we're walking in,
   We're walking in together,
   Join hands and back again,
   Together here we go!

4. Now take your partner's arm
   And swing around together,
   Now take your partner's arm,
   Together, here we go!

May I?

WORDS AND MUSIC
BY ROSE MARIE COOPER

Half-past one, almost two,
Mother dear, what shall I do?

Half-past two, almost three,
You can hop right up to me.

Half-past three, almost four,
I may soon knock at your door.

Half-past four, almost five,
I'll catch you when you arrive.

— ROPE JUMP

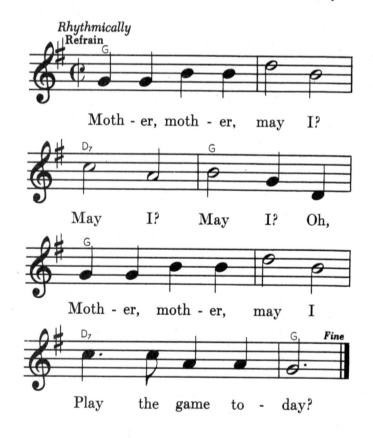

Rhythmically
Refrain

Moth - er, moth - er, may I?

May I? May I? Oh,

Moth - er, moth - er, may I

Play the game to - day?

One child should be chosen to be the mother.
Then the rest of the class forms a single line
and faces her. Everyone sings the refrain.

Verse

G

Take a giant step for - ward,

C   D₇

Then a giant step back, ___

G

A scis - sors and a walk,

C

And a ba - by and a jump,

D₇   G   *D. C. al Fine*

With ev - 'ry - bod - y sing - ing, Oh,

In the first two lines of the verse,
the words of the song tell what to do.

Scissors—cross the right leg in front of the left.
Walk—return the right leg so that feet are parallel.
Baby—cross your arms and pretend to rock a baby.
Jump—jump lightly in place.

Repeat the refrain. While singing it, the mother
will point to a child who becomes the next mother.

Seven Steps

WORDS ADAPTED BY FLORENCE MARTIN
GERMAN FOLK SONG

To find out more about this
time signature, look on
page 95 in your book.

Lively

One, two, three, four, five, six, run! Then re - turn, have
Eins, zwei, drei, vier, fünf, sechs, sieb'n. Eins, zwei, drei, vier,

lots of fun. Run right in, run right out,
fünf, sechs, sieb'n. Eins, zwei, drei, Eins, zwei, drei,

With your part - ner turn a - bout Run right in,
Eins, zwei, drei, vier, fünf, sechs, sieb'n. Eins, zwei, drei,

run right out, With your part - ner turn a - bout.
Eins, zwei, drei, Eins, zwei, drei, vier, fünf, sechs, sieb'n.

Playing rhythm patterns will help you keep a steady beat.

While half the class plays this pattern:

The other half may play this pattern:

Put these two patterns together and you will hear a steady flow of eighth notes.

20

Bicycle Built for Two

Pretend that you are
pedaling a bike while
you sing this song.

WORDS AND MUSIC
BY HARRY DACRE

Liltingly

1. Dai - sy, Dai - sy, Give me your an - swer, do. ____
2. Mi - chael, Mi - chael, Here is your an - swer true. ____

I'm half cra - zy, All for the love of you. ____
You're half cra - zy, If you think that will do. ____

It won't be a sty - lish mar - riage, ___ I can't af -
If you can't af - ford a car - riage, ___ There won't be

ford a car - riage, ___ But you'll look sweet up -
an - y mar - riage, ___ For I'll be switched if

on the seat Of a bi - cy - cle built for two. ____
I'll get hitched On a bi - cy - cle built for two. ____

Pop, Goes the Weasel!

TRADITIONAL AMERICAN SONG

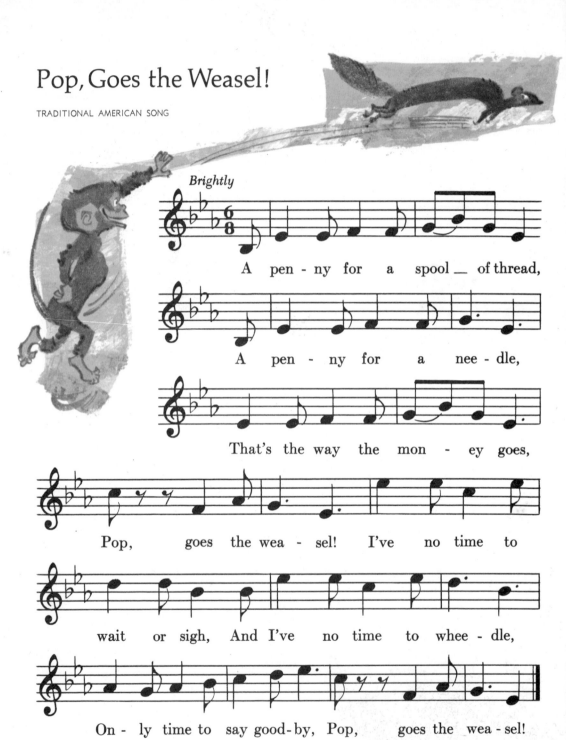

Brightly

A pen - ny for a spool — of thread,

A pen - ny for a nee - dle,

That's the way the mon - ey goes,

Pop, goes the wea - sel! I've no time to

wait or sigh, And I've no time to whee - dle,

On - ly time to say good-by, Pop, goes the wea - sel!

22

2. Oh, all around the chicken
      coop
   The monkey chased the weasel,
   That's the way the money
      goes,
   Pop, goes the weasel!
   I've no time to wait or sigh,
   And I've no time to wheedle,
   Only time to say goodby.
   Pop, goes the weasel!

Hokey Pokey

AMERICAN PLAY PARTY SONG

Easily

You put your right foot in, __ You take your right foot out, __

You put your right foot in __ And shake it all a - bout,

And then you do the hok - ey pok - ey And you

turn your - self a - bout, And that's what it's all a - bout. *Hey!*

Hiking Through the Country

WORDS BY G. K. EVANS
GERMAN FOLK TUNE

Briskly

Hik - ing through the coun-try wide, Juch-hei-di, juch-hei-da,

With my com-rades by my side, Juch-hei-di, hei-da.

Up the hill and down the glen, Far a - way and back a - gain,

Juch-hei-di, hei-di, hei-da, Juch-hei-di, juch-hei-da,

Juch-hei-di, hei-di, hei-da, Juch-hei-di, hei-da.

Here are two rhythm patterns you can tap as you sing.

What simple patterns can you make up
to play on rhythm instruments
as you sing this song?

Sugar Bush

WORDS AND MUSIC
BY JOSEF MARAIS

1. Su - gar   bush, come dance with me,

Let   the   oth - er   fel - lows be.

Dance the *vas - trap* mer - ri - ly,

Su - gar   bush, come dance with   me.

2. Sugar bush, I love you so, *(Clap)*
   I will never let you go. *(Clap)*
   Don't you let your mother know, *(Clap)*
   Sugar bush, I love you so.

Hop Up, My Ladies!

AMERICAN FOLK SONG

Tap or clap this pattern as you sing:

Happily

Verse

1. Did you ev - er go to meet - ing, Un - cle Joe, Un - cle Joe? Did you ev - er go to meet - ing, Un - cle Joe? __ Did you ev - er go to meet - ing, Un - cle Joe, Un - cle Joe? Don't mind the weath - er, so the wind don't blow.

2. Will your horse carry double, Uncle Joe, Uncle Joe? *(3 times)*
Don't mind the weather, so the wind don't blow.

26

Refrain

Hop up, my la - dies, three in a row,

Hop up, my la - dies, three in a row,

Hop up, my la - dies, three in a row,

Don't mind the weath - er, so the wind don't blow.

3. Is your horse a single-footer, Uncle Joe, Uncle Joe? *(3 times)*
Don't mind the weather, so the wind don't blow.

Willowbee

SOUTHERN SINGING GAME

You might sing this pattern quietly as an introduction and all through the song.

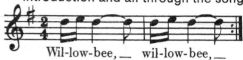

Wil-low-bee, — wil-low-bee, —

Moderately

This way you wil - low - bee, Oh, wil - low - bee,

Oh, wil - low - bee, — This way you wil - low - bee, —

All night ____ long. Oh, ____

1. Walk - ing
2. Skip - ping } down the al - ley, al - ley, al - ley,

Walk - ing
Skip - ping } down the al - ley, all night long. Oh, —

What kind of notes are these?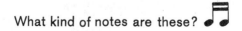

28

If you make up a dance
to go with this song,
will it be fast or slow?

Pick a Bale of Cotton

SOUTHERN FOLK SONG

Vigorously

1. You got to jump down, turn a-round, pick a bale of cot - ton,
2. Oh, me and my part - ner ___ can pick a bale of cot - ton,

Jump down, turn a - round, Pick a bale a day.

Oh, Man - dy, pick a bale of cot - ton,

Oh, Man - dy, pick a bale a day!

3. I went to Alabama
   To pick a bale of cotton,
   Jump down, turn around,
   Pick a bale a day.
   Oh, Mandy, pick a bale of cotton,
   Oh, Mandy, pick a bale a day!

29

The Dancing Lesson

FROM "HANSEL AND GRETEL"
BY ENGELBERT HUMPERDINCK

Lively

GRETEL: Broth- er, come and dance with me,

Both my hands I of - fer thee;

Right foot first, left foot then,

'Round a - bout and back a - gain.

GRETEL: With your feet you tap, tap, tap,
HANSEL: With your head you nick, nick, nick,

How many different rhythm patterns
can you find in this song?

With your hands you clap, clap, clap, Right foot first,
With your fin - gers click, click, click, Right foot first,

left foot then, 'Round a - bout and back a - gain.
left foot then, 'Round a - bout and back a - gain.

Hansel and Gretel Overture

FROM "HANSEL AND GRETEL"
AN OPERA BY ENGELBERT HUMPERDINCK

"Hansel and Gretel" is an opera about a boy and girl who become lost in the forest and are caught by a wicked witch. The witch has already turned many children into gingerbread. She tries to bake Hansel and Gretel, but they trick her and push her into the oven.

The Overture is played before the opera begins. It gives you some idea of what will happen later.

As you listen to the first melody, you can picture Hansel and Gretel in the dark forest.

Later you hear this melody. It is the Gingerbread Children.

Poll Perico

WORDS BY MARY W. DUTRE
CHILEAN FOLK TUNE

Here is a pattern
to tap or clap
as you sing this song:

Gaily

1. Poll Pe - ri - co is a pol - ly Who is nev - er mel - an -
2. On his perch the par - rot proud - ly Will re - peat a word so

chol - y. He is full of fun and laugh - ter,
loud - ly! This he does to get at - ten - tion,

Refrain

All day long and some-times aft - er.
So be care - ful what you men - tion. Bright feath - ered

fel - low, Red, green, and yel - low, Gay Poll Pe -

ri - co, Bel - lo am - i - go! i - go!

Bello amigo means good friend in Spanish.

32

MELODY IN MUSIC

Blue Bells of Scotland

WORDS BY ANNIE McVICAR
SCOTTISH FOLK TUNE

Moderately

1. Oh, where, tell me where is your — High-land lad - die gone?
2. Oh, where, tell me where did your — High-land lad - die dwell?

He's gone wi' stream - ing ban - ners where —
He dwelt in bon - ny Scot - land, where —

no - ble deeds are done; And it's oh, in my
blooms the sweet blue - bell; And it's oh, in my

heart I _____ wish him safe at home.
heart I _____ lo'e my lad - die well.

Hike Along

WORDS BY FLORENCE MARTIN
HUNGARIAN FOLK TUNE

Cheerfully

d min.

1. Take your pack and let's go hik - ing!
Through the woods and by the riv - er,

A₇   d min. *Fine*

O - ver __ hill __ and __ field we go!
On __ a __ path __ we're __ sure to know!

g min.   D₇   g min.

Sing - ing, sing - ing as we hike a - long;

C₇   F   A₇, *D. C.*

Hik - ing, hik - ing to a hap - py song!

2. Following now the river's turning,
We are on a winding ridge.
Singing, singing as we hike along;
Hiking, hiking to a happy song!
Now the pathway seems to widen
As we near the old footbridge.

34

My Island Home

WORDS BY T. V. VELOTTA
PHILIPPINE MELODY

Peacefully

1. My is - land home knows the sea and the foam,
2. My hut, though small, is ___ stur - dy and tall,

And the tall su - gar cane grow - ing o - ver the plain;
And I see from my room love - ly flow - ers in bloom;

A trop - ic breeze stirs the co - co - nut trees,
The boats each day come ___ in from the bay,

And hap - py am I 'neath the blue sky.
To rest on the sand of my is - land.

The Lonely Dove

WORDS BY MARIA PONS
WELSH MELODY

Notice the bell part
written above the melody.
It uses only two notes.

Can you make up another
using these two notes?

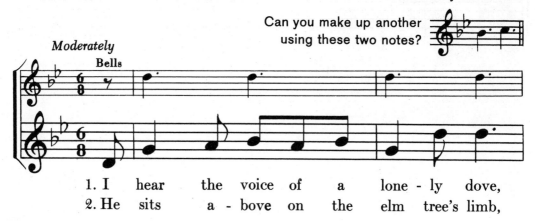

Moderately

1. I hear the voice of a lone - ly dove,
2. He sits a - bove on the elm tree's limb,

Coo - roo - roo, the notes are so clear;
Coo - roo - roo, he sings sweet and slow;

He sings a song to his la - dy love,
And soon his la - dy love an - swers him,

To tell her he'll al - ways be near. _____
Re - peat - ing his song, soft and low. _____

Clouds

WORDS BY JOHN ANDREWS
MUSIC BY FRANZ SCHUBERT

Does this melody start on a
strong beat? How do you know?

Smoothly

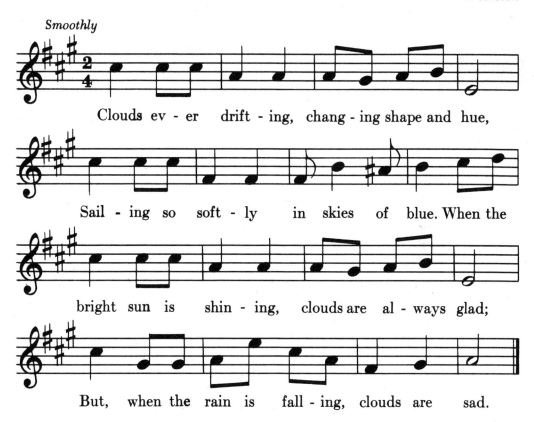

Clouds ev - er drift - ing, chang - ing shape and hue,

Sail - ing so soft - ly in skies of blue. When the

bright sun is shin - ing, clouds are al - ways glad;

But, when the rain is fall - ing, clouds are sad.

Merry May the Keel Row

WORDS BY JAMES HOGG
SCOTCH FOLK SONG

Rhythmically

1. As   I came down the Can - on - gate,
2. He   wears __ a   blue bon - net,

the Can - on - gate, the Can - on - gate,
blue bon - net, blue bon - net,

As   I   came down the Can - on - gate,
A   snow-white rose up - on __ it,

I   heard   a   las - sie   sing.
a   dim - ple   in   his   chin.

Refrain

Oh,
And, } mer - ry may the   keel   row,

the keel row, the keel ___ row;

Oh, mer - ry may the keel row

the ship that my love's in.

Mer - ry may the keel row, the keel row,

the keel ___ row: Oh, mer - ry may the

keel row the ship that my love's in.

This is My Father's World

WORDS BY MALTBIE D. BABCOCK
MUSIC BY FRANKLIN L. SHEPPARD

Moderately

1. This __ is my Fa - ther's world, And __ to my list - 'ning
2. This __ is my Fa - ther's world, Oh, __ let me ne'er for-

ears, All na - ture sings and __ round me rings The
get That though the wrong seems __ oft so strong, God

mu - sic of the __ spheres. This is my Fa - ther's world;
is __ the Ru - ler __ yet. This is my Fa - ther's world;

I __ rest me in the thought Of rocks and trees,
Why __ should my heart be sad? The Lord is King;

of __ skies and seas; His hand __ the won - ders __ wrought.
let the heav - ens ring! God reigns; __ let the earth be __ glad!

Fairest Lord Jesus

TRADITIONAL CRUSADER'S HYMN

There are four phrases
in this song. Are any
of them alike?

Reverently

1. Fair - est Lord Je - sus, Ru - ler of all na - ture,
2. Fair are the mead - ows, Fair - er still the wood - lands,

O Thou of God and ___ man the son;
Robed in the bloom - ing ___ garb of spring;

Thee will I cher - ish, Thee will I hon - or,
Je - sus is fair - er, Je - sus is pur - er,

Thou my soul's glo - ry, joy, and crown.
Who makes the woe - ful heart to sing.

3. Fair is the sunshine, Fairer still the moonlight,
   And all the twinkling starry host;
   Jesus shines brighter, Jesus shines purer
   Than all the angels heav'n can boast.

41

For a Leaf

WORDS BY MADELEINE A. DUFAY
MUSIC BY W. A. MOZART

Smoothly

1. For a leaf, there's a tree, ___ for a
2. For a bird, there are skies, ___ from the

wave, there's the sea, ___ And the night when it's
plains, moun-tains rise, ___ Great or small, God has

fad - ing sees a sun - beam's ten - der light.
giv - en of His boun - ty to us all.

This is the Wind

WORDS BY ESTHER DAVIS AND RUTH DE CESARE
MUSIC BY RUTH DE CESARE

Lightly

This is the wind, the wind, the wind;

This is the wind of au - tumn.

1. It nips your ears as it puffs and
2. It tells the leaves, "Come and fly with

blows, Creeps through your shoes as it
me; Come all you leaves down from

tweaks your nose, Call - ing old
ev - 'ry tree, All of the

win - ter with its snows.
birds are gone, you see."

This is the wind of au - tumn.

The Sandman

WORDS ADAPTED
MUSIC BY JOHANNES BRAHMS

1. The flow - ers all sleep sound - ly be - neath the moon so bright; They nod their heads to - geth - er and dream all through the night. The sway - ing trees move to and fro, and

2. The sandman will be coming
   To find each sleepy head,
   He knows that little children
   Should be asleep in bed.
   And gently he will close the eyes
   Of each drowsy child he spies.
   Schlafe, schlafe,
   Close your eyes, *mein Kindelein.*

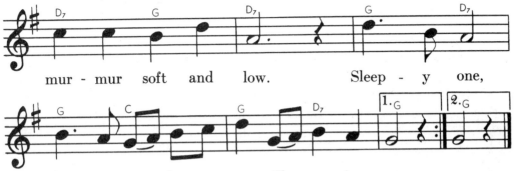

mur - mur   soft   and   low.   Sleep - y   one,

sleep - y   one, _ close your eyes till _ morn-ing   comes.   comes.

Träumerei

BY ROBERT SCHUMANN

"Träumerei" means dreams or reveries. This piece is part of a collection of pieces called "Scenes from Childhood." As you might expect, the melody is calm and peaceful.

Does the melody move mostly by step or skip?

Some of the other titles in the collection are "Knight of the Hobby Horse," "The Curious Story," and "At the Hearth." What kind of melody would you write to describe a hobby horse? Would it be smooth or jerky?

Guardian Angels

TRADITIONAL WORDS
MUSIC BY ROBERT SCHUMANN

Slowly

1. When chil - dren lay them down to sleep, Loo loo loo loo,
2. When morn - ing light be - gins to break, La la la la,

Bright an - gels come their watch to keep, Loo loo loo loo,
And chil - dren from their sleep a - wake, La la la la,

Cov - er them up, all safe - ly and warm,
Still at their side and all through the day,

Loo loo, Ten - der - ly shield them from ev - 'ry harm.
La la, An - gels keep guard as they work and play.

Robert Schumann wrote many songs for his children. He may have
written this song to be sung as a lullaby when they were going
to sleep. It should be sung very quietly and smoothly.

At the Gate of Heaven

WORDS ADAPTED
SPANISH FOLK MELODY

Smoothly

1. At the gate of heav'n, ti - ny shoes they are giv - ing
2. An - gel choirs in heav'n, with their voi - ces, are bring - ing

To the lit - tle bare - foot - ed an - gels, there liv - ing.
Joy - ous songs of love; all for thee they are ring - ing.

Slum - ber, my lit - tle one, Slum - ber, my lit - tle one,

Slum - ber, my *ni - ño,* a - *rru,* a - *rru.*

47

Shalom A'leychem

ISRAELI SONG

What does the time signature of this song tell you? Look on page 94 for another way to write this time signature.

Brightly

To you we bring peace - ful greet - ings, ____
He - ve - nu sha - lom a' - ley - chem, ____

To you we bring peace - ful greet - ings, ____
He - ve - nu sha - lom a' - ley - chem, ____

To you we bring ____ peace - ful greet - ings, ____
He - ve - nu sha - lom a' - ley - chem, ____

We bring our greet - ings, greet - ings, greet - ings now of peace.
He - ve - nu sha - lom, sha - lom, sha - lom a' - ley - chem.

There are four phrases in the melody of this song. The four phrases are alike in many ways. Each phrase has the same text. Each phrase starts with the melody going up. Can you find some other ways in which they are alike?

48

Down in the Valley

KENTUCKY MOUNTAIN SONG

$\frac{9}{8}$ time swings in threes.

Moderately

1. Down in the val - ley, the val - ley so low,
2. Ro - ses love sun - shine, ____ vio - lets love dew,

Hang your head o - ver, hear the wind blow,
An - gels in heav - en know I love you.

Hear the wind blow, dear, hear the wind blow,
Know I love you, dear, know I love you,

Hang your head o - ver, hear the wind blow.
An - gels in heav - en know I love you.

3. If you don't love me, none else will do,
   My heart is breaking, dear, just for you.
   Breaking for you, dear, breaking for you,
   My heart is breaking, dear, just for you.

Drum and Fiddle

TRADITIONAL

Clarinet

The tone of the clarinet is produced by a reed vibrating against the back of the mouthpiece. This reed is made of a thin piece of cane. Unlike the trumpet mouthpiece, which fits against the lips, the clarinet mouthpiece fits between the player's lips.

The pitch is changed by using metal keys which open or close holes bored in the instrument.

RANGE *8va*

Clarinet
mouthpiece:

The clarinet is often used as a melody instrument. Its tone is dark and mellow in the lower and middle parts of the range, but rather piercing and brilliant in the upper part. Fast passages and skips can be played on the clarinet almost as easily as they can be played on the violin. A symphony orchestra will usually use two or three clarinets.

Trumpet

The tone of the trumpet is produced by the vibrations of the player's lips in a mouthpiece. This mouthpiece is shaped like a small cup. Different pitches are played by changing the tension of the lips and by using the three valves.

RANGE

Trumpet mouthpiece

At one time, the trumpet was a long, straight tube. It was discovered that the trumpet could be more easily handled and played if the tubing were bent. Before the three valves were added, only a few tones could be played on the trumpet. The valves change the tube's length and make it possible for the player to produce all the notes of any scale.

The trumpet has a bright, brilliant tone and is seldom used as a solo instrument. There are two or three trumpets in a symphony orchestra.

Violin

The violin is held under the chin and played either with a bow which is drawn across the strings, or by plucking the strings with the fingers. The pitch is changed by shortening the length of the string with the finger.

RANGE *8va*

The violin strings are tuned to:

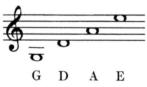

G   D   A   E

The violin can express many moods. It can give voice to a thread of sound or a warm, singing tone as expressive as the human voice. However, singers can not sing with such agility or cover such a wide range.

Because such a wide variety of sounds can be produced on the violin, and since the tone quality is pleasant to listen to for long periods of time, the violins are used for playing the melodies of a piece more often than any other orchestral instrument. It is not unusual to find thirty or more violins in a large orchestra.

Tirilin

WORDS BY LUCILLE WOOD
MEXICAN FOLK TUNE

Rhythmically
Maracas and Woodblocks

(Continue throughout)

1. I like to sing, ti - ri - lin, ti - ri - lin,
2. A vi - o - lin, ti - ri - lin, ti - ri - lin,

A danc - ing song, to - ro - lon, to - ro - lon;
A slide trom - bone, to - ro - lon, to - ro - lon;

I like to sing, ti - ri - lin, ti - ri - lin,
A vi - o - lin, ti - ri - lin, ti - ri - lin,

A danc - ing song, to - ro - lon, to - ro - lon.
A slide trom - bone, to - ro - lon, to - ro - lon.

3. A piccolo, ti-ri-lo, ti-ri-lo,
   A big bass drum, ta-ta-tum, ta-ta-tum;
   A piccolo, ti-ri-lo, ti-ri-lo,
   A big bass drum, ta-ta-tum, ta-ta-tum.

La la la la la la la la la la, La la la

la la la la la la la, La la la la la la la la la

1. la, La la la la, _____ 2. la, La la la la. _____

Bass Drum

The drum was undoubtedly one of the earliest instruments. In the orchestra and band, the bass drum is often used to accent the main pulse of the music. Sudden dramatic effects, like the crash of thunder, can be played easily and effectively on the bass drum.

The bass drum is made of a round wooden shell over which two playing heads have been stretched tightly. The sound is produced when one of the heads is struck with a stick. This stick has a large ball of felt or wool at the striking end.

Trumpet and Drum

FROM "JEUX D'ENFANTS"
BY GEORGES BIZET

"Trumpet and Drum" is from a collection of short pieces called "Children's Games." This piece is about children pretending they are marching soldiers.

Here is the main melody of the march. How many times do you hear it? Listen carefully for the trumpet fanfares that are heard all through the piece. Do they make the music sound more military?

Hens and Cocks

FROM "CARNIVAL OF ANIMALS"
BY CAMILLE SAINT-SAENS

Composers often write music that is a picture in sound. They may write about things such as the sea, or clouds, or animals. In this piece, Saint-Saens wrote music showing a flock of chickens as they cackle and cluck.

This is the melody of the chickens. What instrument plays it?

Saint-Saens also wrote music describing other animals. Some of the other pieces are about turtles, a kangaroo, and an elephant.

56

POETRY AND MUSIC

A Dream

WORDS AND MUSIC
BY LUCILE HULTQUIST

Softly

I dreamed one night that I could fly

And soared and cir - cled in the ___ sky;

And when I woke up in my ___ bed,

There was a feath - er by my head.

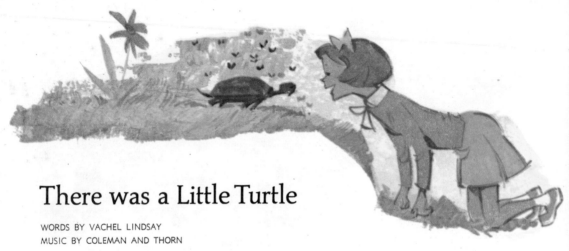

There was a Little Turtle

WORDS BY VACHEL LINDSAY
MUSIC BY COLEMAN AND THORN

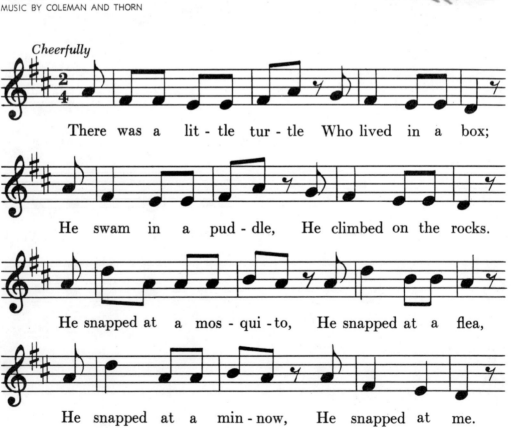

Cheerfully

There was a lit - tle tur - tle Who lived in a box;

He swam in a pud - dle, He climbed on the rocks.

He snapped at a mos - qui - to, He snapped at a flea,

He snapped at a min - now, He snapped at me.

He caught the mos - qui - to, He caught the flea,

He caught the min - now, But he did - n't catch me!

This song uses two different
time signatures. Some measures
have three beats and some have four.

Spiders

WORDS BY AILEEN FISHER
MUSIC BY MARY WHITCOMB

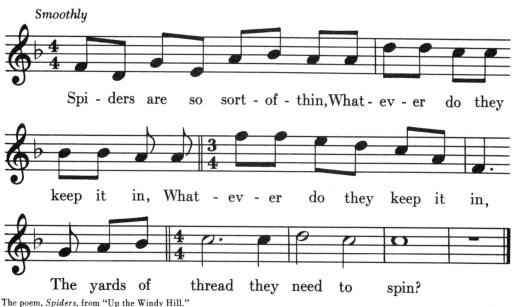

Smoothly

Spi - ders are so sort - of - thin, What - ev - er do they

keep it in, What - ev - er do they keep it in,

The yards of thread they need to spin?

Wonderful World

WORDS BY WILLIAM B. RANDS
MUSIC BY MADELEINE A. DUFAY

Liltingly

Great, wide won - der - ful world, With the won - der - ful

wa - ter round you curled, And the won - der - ful

grass up - on your breast, World, you are beau - ti - f'ly

dressed! Won - der - ful world, how far do you go?

With the wheat fields that nod, and the riv - ers that

flow, With cit - ies and gar - dens and cliffs and isles,

And peo - ple up - on you for thou-sands of miles!

This song is written with three beats in each measure.
However, it moves along quickly and you feel only one swing in each measure.

O Father, Lift Our Hearts to Thee

IRISH HYMN

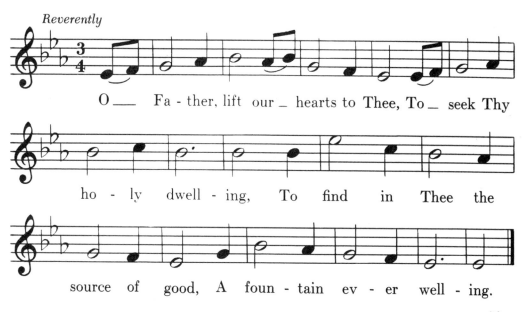

Reverently

O __ Fa - ther, lift our __ hearts to Thee, To __ seek Thy

ho - ly dwell - ing, To find in Thee the

source of good, A foun - tain ev - er well - ing.

Marching Song

WORDS BY R. L. STEVENSON
MUSIC BY MARY BECK STEVENS

Two measures of this song use
only the tones of the I chord.
Can you find these measures?

Steadily

Tr rum 2 3 4! 1 2 3 4!

Forward 2 3 4! March 2 3 4!

F   C₇
Bring   a   comb and play up - on   it,
Mar - y   Jane com-mands the par - ty,

F
March - ing   here   we   come;
Pe - ter   leads   the   rear;

Bb   F
Wil - lie   cocks his High - land bon - net,
Feet in   time, a - lert and heart - y,

62

Johnnie beats the drum. *(Beat!)*

Each a grenadier.

All in the most martial manner, Marching double quick;

While the napkin, like a banner, Waves upon the stick.

Here's enough of fame and pillage, Great commander Jane,

Now that we've been 'round the village, Let's go home again.

Cradle Song

WORDS BY H. R. WILSON
MUSIC BY FRANZ SCHUBERT

Look on page 96 to see
how a slur affects a melody.

Slowly

1. Slum - ber, slum - ber, ten - der lit - tle __ flow - er,
2. Slum - ber, slum - ber, lit - tle fad - ed __ flow - er,

Moth - er's lov - ing care doth a - round __ thee __ twine;
Still doth moth - er's love a - round __ thee __ glow;

Sweet and rest - ful be _____ this hour, ___
It is thy ___ pro - tect - ing pow'r, ___

Sooth - ing fall __ this lull - a - by __ of __ mine.
Guard - ing thee __ where e'er thy feet __ may __ go.

3. Slumber, slumber, little angel flower,
   Gently, gently dreaming on and on
   Sweetly as a rosy bower;
   May God hold thee till the coming dawn.

Now the Day is Over

WORDS BY SABINE BARING-GOULD
MUSIC BY J. BARNBY

Smoothly

1. Now the day is o - ver,
2. Through the hours of dark - ness,

Night is draw - ing nigh,
May Thine an - gels spread

Shad - ows of the eve - ning
Their white wings a - bove me,

Steal a - cross the sky.
Watch - ing 'round my bed.

The mood of this song is quiet and restful.
Although the melody moves very little, the
accompaniment adds interest and color.

65

Come, Little Leaves

ANONYMOUS
MUSIC BY J. H. CLEMMER

The skips in this melody
remind us of the leaves as
they skip over the ground.

Moderately

1. "Come, lit - tle leaves," said the wind one day,
2. Soon all the leaves heard the wind's low call,

"O - ver the mead - ow with me and play,
Down they came flut - ter - ing, one and all.

Put on your dress - es of green and gold, For
O - ver the brown fields they danced and flew,

sum - mer is gone and the days __ grow cold."_____
Sing - ing the gay lit - tle songs __ they knew._____

3. Dancing and whirling the little leaves went,
Winter had called them and they were content.
Soon fast asleep in their earthly beds,
Snow laid a coverlet o'er their heads.

In Our Rocket

WORDS AND MUSIC
BY RUTH DE CESARE

Gaily

We will rock-et to the moon some day, And catch a star as it pass-es, while we're flash-ing by. When our rock-et's read-y and our course is stead-y, We'll see a new world some-where in the sky.

Leron

WORDS ADAPTED BY FLORENCE MARTIN
PHILIPPINE FOLK TUNE

Play this rhythm on
maracas and sticks:

Liltingly

A lit - tle boy, Le - ron,

Climbed high up in a tree,

To pick some pa - pay - a,

And bring them down to me.

2. This chipper little lad
Who fell and bumped his head,
He didn't stop to cry,
But hustled on instead.
He climbed another tree
And, picking carefully,
He filled his basket up
And brought it down to me.

$\frac{2}{4}$ ♩ ♫ ♩ ♫ |

The fruit was ver - y ripe

And clus - tered all a - round;

Le - ron reached out too far

And tum - bled to the ground. __

3. Leron then scampered on
   To join the games and fun.
   But when he had a job,
   He got it quickly done.
   He ran and romped and chased
   Along his merry way.
   This happy little boy
   Had fun at work or play!

The Grasshopper and the Ants

WORDS ADAPTED FROM AESOP
MUSIC BY ALFRED STERN

Gaily

1. Dur - ing the spring, and all sum - mer long,
2. When win - ter came, his food was all gone.

The grass - hop - per sang this sweet lit - tle song:
He went to the ants for food to live on.

"Oh, fa - la - doo, tsk - tsk - tsk, fa - la - doo,

tsk - tsk - tsk, Fa - la - doo, fa - la - doo day." __

3. "You've much to learn," the ants gravely said,
   "For everyone has to earn his own bread."

4. "We saw you dance the summer away
   While we worked and saved for this win'try day."

70

Winter Lullaby

WORDS BY LUCILE HULTQUIST
RUSSIAN FOLK SONG

Peacefully

1. Soon the win - ter dusk will deep - en,
   Glit - ter - ing like frost - y crys - tals,

And the moon will rise.
Stars will fill the skies.

Lit - tle one, it's time for slum - ber,

Close your drow - sy eyes.

2. Black and silent stand the fir trees
   In the winter night;
   But, inside, the logs are glowing,
   Flames are burning bright.
   Sleep, my baby, warm and cozy,
   Till the morning light.

Little Bird

TRANS. BY ETHEL CROWNINSHIELD
MEXICAN FOLK MELODY

How many times do you find
this pattern in the song?

Lightly

Rhythm
Instruments

(Continue throughout)

1. Lit - tle bird, would you be go - ing?
2. Lit - tle bird, you'll soon be soar - ing

Lit - tle   bird, would you be know - ing,   Far out - side,
Where the   sun - shine now is pour - ing, Though your cage

soft winds are blow-ing,   Far out-side, bright flow'rs are grow-ing.
is bright and shin-ing,   For the out - doors you are pin - ing.

Refrain

Can - ta,   lit - tle   bird,   some - one   is   near   you,

Can - ta,   lit - tle   bird,   some - one   will   hear   you,

Can - ta,   lit - tle   bird,   some - one will   see   you,

Can - ta,   lit - tle   bird,   some - one will   free   you.

Dance of the Mosquito

BY ANATOL LIADOV

When the music starts, you can hear the mosquito as it buzzes through the air. Here is the melody of the mosquito. Can you tell what instrument plays it?

This melody is played twice. How does the composer change the sound of the tune when it is played the second time? Can you find any repeated patterns in the melody?

Here is a rhythm pattern you can play on a triangle or on sand blocks. Play the notes very lightly.

73

So Long, Mary

WORDS AND MUSIC
BY GEORGE M. COHAN

Here is one rhythm pattern
used in this song:

What other pattern can you
find in several places?

Liltingly

So long, Mar-y! Mar-y, we will miss you so; ___

So long, Mar-y! How we hate to see you go;

And we'll all be long-ing for you, Mar-y,

While you roam. ___ So long, Mar-y,

Don't for-get to come back home!

PLAYING INSTRUMENTS

Canoe Song

AMERICAN INDIAN SONG

Cheerfully

1. My pad - dle's keen and bright, Flash-ing with sil - ver;

Fol - low the wild goose flight, Dip, dip, and swing.

2. Dip, dip and swing her back,
   Flashing with silver;
   Swift as the wild goose flies,
   Dip, dip and swing.

From "Adventures in Song," © 1947 by Cooperative
Recreation Service Inc., Delaware, Ohio.

Oranges and Lemons

ENGLISH FOLK SONG

"Oran - ges and lem - ons," say the bells of St. Clem - ents.
"Give me five far - things," say the bells of St. Mar - tins";

"When will you pay me?" say the bells of Old Bai - ley;

"When I grow rich," say the bells of Shore - ditch.

"When will that be?" __ say the bells of Step - ney; __

"I do not know," __ says the great bell of Bow. __

Here comes the can - dle to __ light you to bed,

And here is your pil - low to __ cov - er your head.

Drum-de-dum

WORDS AND MUSIC
BY JOAN GARDNER AND ADELAIDE HALPERN

Make up a drum part to play
as you sing this song.

Lively

I can play a drum - de-dum - dum - dum,
When I play a drum - de-dum - dum - dum,

And I love to drum - de- dum-dum-dum. I
My heart beats so drum - de- dum-dum-dum. When

drum - de - dum - dum on a chair, I drum - de-dum-dum
I get old - er, I will play ___ in a band some

1. ev - 'ry - where; I can feel the mu - sic in the air.

2. day, Be - cause I love to drum. ___

Side by Side

WORDS BY MARTHA HARRIS
MUSIC BY JUDITH EISENSTEIN

Vigorously

Side by side, ___ we're march-ing side by side, ___

We're al - ways full of pep, all in step.

Watch us as we hit our stride,

Fast or slow, here we go!

Side by side, watch us as we hit our stride!

Grandma Said

WORDS BY YVONNE CARR
FRENCH FOLK TUNE

Pretend that you are
playing each of the
instruments you sing about.

1. Grand - ma said, "To town we'll go, We will get a
2. Grand - ma said, "Please do not mourn, We will get a

new ban - jo." But the ban - jo goes plunk, plunk, Plunk - y,
new brass horn." But the horn goes root, toot, toot, Root - y,

plunk - y, plunk, plunk, plunk. Hear our ban - jo plunk, plunk, plunk.
toot - y, root, toot, toot. Oh, the root - y, toot - y horn.

3. Grandma said, "Now you must come,
   We will get a little drum."
   But the drum goes dum, da-dum,
   Dum-da, dum-da, dum, dum, dum.
   Oh, the noisy little drum.

4. Grandma said, "Oh, this won't do,
   We'll find a baton for you."
   The baton goes swish-swish-swish,
   Swishy-swishy, swish-swish-swish.
   It's the best to listen to.

She Watched Her Sheep

WORDS BY ADELE ST. ETIENNE
FRENCH FOLK MELODY

Gaily

1. She watched her sheep while play - ing Up - on her drum,
Elle é - tait une ber - gè - re, Et ron, ron, ron,

with a rum - tum-tum. She watched her sheep while play - ing
pe - tit pa - ta - pon. Elle é - tait une ber - gè - re,

Up - on her lit - tle drum, tum-tum,
Qui gar - dait ses mou -tons, ron, ron,

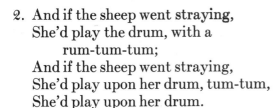

Up - on her lit - tle drum. ___
Qui gar - dait ses mou - tons. ___

2. And if the sheep went straying,
  She'd play the drum, with a
      rum-tum-tum;
  And if the sheep went straying,
  She'd play upon her drum, tum-tum,
  She'd play upon her drum.

3. They'd come without delaying,
  To hear the drum, with a
      rum-tum-tum;
  They'd come without delaying,
  To hear her little drum, tum-tum,
  To hear her little drum.

81

Hear the Bells

WORDS AND MUSIC
BY RUTH DE CESARE

Make up a bell part for this
song. Use the tones D and A.

Joyfully

Hear the bells a - ring - ing, Lis - ten as they say:

"Health and cheer through the year; For - tune's on its way."

Hear them ring; hear them sing. Here's a fine new day.

We are Fine Musicians

WORDS ADAPTED BY E. J. HERMANN
GERMAN FOLK TUNE

Brightly

Oh, we are fine mu - si - cians, as you can plain - ly see,
All ver - y fine mu - si - cians, we know you will a - gree.

82

1. On the rhy - thm sticks we go tap, tap, tap,
2. On the tam - bou - rines we go rap, rap, rap,
3. On the tri - an - gles we go ding, ding, ding,

On the rhy - thm sticks we go tap, tap, tap.
On the tam - bou - rines we go rap, rap, rap.
On the tri - an - gles we go ding, ding, ding.

Voices only

Now all to - geth - er!

Voices and instruments   *Verses accumulate*

With a tap, tap, tap, and a tap, tap, tap,
With a rap, rap, rap, and a rap, rap, rap,
With a ding, ding, ding, and a ding, ding, ding,

All fine mu - si - cians!

Through the Winter Night

WORDS BY CLAUDIA REGEN
GERMAN FOLK TUNE

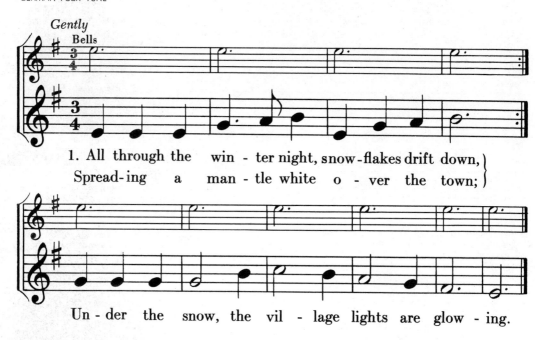

1. All through the win - ter night, snow-flakes drift down,
Spread-ing a man - tle white o - ver the town;

Un - der the snow, the vil - lage lights are glow - ing.

2. Over the countryside, cov'ring the ground,
   Snow crystals gently glide, making no sound;
   Under the snow, the seeds of spring are growing.

I'd Like to be in Texas

TRADITIONAL COWBOY SONG

I can see the cat - tle graz - ing o'er the

84

hills at ear - ly morn; I can see the camp - fires

smok - ing at the break - ing of the dawn.

I can hear the bron - cos neigh - ing, I can

hear the cow - boys sing; I'd — like to be in

Tex - as for the round - up in the spring. —

Down in a Coalmine

TRADITIONAL

You may have fun acting
out digging and mining coal
as you sing this song.

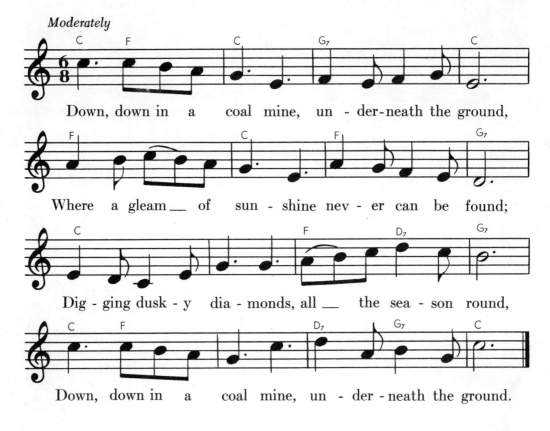

Down, down in a coal mine, un - der-neath the ground,

Where a gleam __ of sun - shine nev - er can be found;

Dig - ging dusk - y dia - monds, all __ the sea - son round,

Down, down in a coal mine, un - der - neath the ground.

Here are two rhythm patterns for
you to play. Can you make up a
third pattern for the triangle?

READING MUSIC

Are You Sleeping?

FRENCH FOLK TUNE

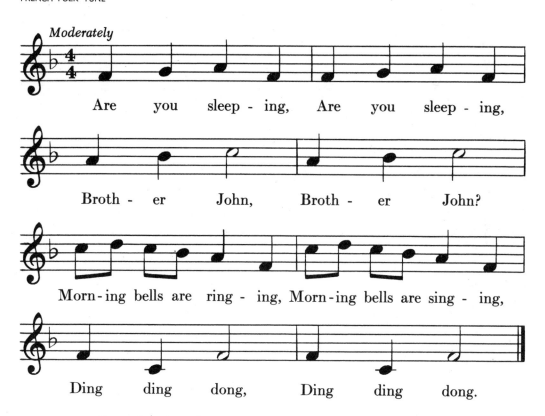

Moderately

Are you sleep - ing, Are you sleep - ing,

Broth - er John, Broth - er John?

Morn-ing bells are ring - ing, Morn-ing bells are sing - ing,

Ding ding dong, Ding ding dong.

Sing this familiar song.

There are many quarter notes (♩) in this song.

Which notes are shorter? Which notes are longer?

This is one pattern that is repeated in this song:

How many other repeated patterns can you find?

The Bells

TRADITIONAL

The home tone of this song is C.
Does it start on the home tone?

Home tone: C
Starting note: C (*do*, 1)

Rhythmically

All   the   bells   are   gai - ly   ring - ing,   Bing,   bong,   bing,   bong,

Call - ing   us   to   hear   them   sing - ing,   Bing,   bong,   bong.

You have learned that a scale is like a stairway.
Does this song move up or down the scale? How many times?
Sing the song with syllables, and again with numbers.

You will see that the bottom C in this song is placed on a *leger line*. Leger lines are added to the staff to locate notes which are above or below the staff.

To play the C major scale
    on the piano,
look at this picture and find the keys that match those having letter names.

Some may play the piano, others may play the scale on bells, while others sing the letter names of the C major scale. Listen as you sing or play.

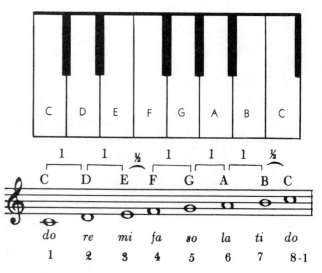

88

A *major scale* has half steps between 3—4, and 7—8.

You can play a *half step* on the piano
by playing any two keys which are
exactly *next to each other*.
Such keys do not have a key between.

All other scale steps are whole steps.
A whole step is made up of two half steps.
You can play a whole step by playing
any two keys *that have a key between*.

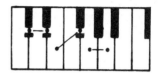

"On St. Paul's Steeple" is built on the C major scale.
Sing the song with both syllables and numbers.
Between what syllables
or numbers are half steps found?

On St. Paul's Steeple

Home tone: C
Starting note: C (*do*, 1)

TRADITIONAL ENGLISH SONG

Moderately

On   St.   Paul's   stee - ple   stands   a   tree,

As   full   of   ap - ples   as   can   be,

The   lit - tle   boys   of   Lon - don   Town,

They   run   with   hooks   to   pull   them   down.

See if you can read and sing the following songs.

Do do do do ti la so, Do do do do ti la so,
8 8 8 8 7 6 5, 8 8 8 8 7 6 5,

Do do do do ti la so fa mi mi re re do do.
8   8   8   8   7   6   5   4   3   3   2   2   1   1.

To London Town

TRADITIONAL ENGLISH SONG

1. What is the dis - tance to   Lon - don Town pray?
2. There they have cas - tles and   there they have kings;

You could not walk there in man - y   a   day.
There they have thou - sands of won - der - ful things.

Do—mi—so or 1–3–5 are important tones of any scale.

When sounded together, they form a chord:

Since this chord is built on the home tone, or 1, it is called the *I chord.*

Melodies of many songs use the tones of the I chord.
"Tick Tock" is built entirely on the tones of the I chord.

Tick Tock

TRADITIONAL

Steadily

Big clocks mark time slow - ly, tick - tock, tick - tock.

Small clocks mark time fast - er,

tick - tock, tick - tock, tick - tock, tick - tock.

And the lit - tle watch - es mark time

tick - y tock - y, tick - y, tock - y tick - y tock - y tock.

Sing this song with words, numbers, and syllables.
It does not move by step; but by skips and repeated tones.

A melody moves: by step
by skip
by repeated tones.

Yankee Doodle

TRADITIONAL

Read the words of this song
aloud to find out where
the phrases end.

Lively

1. Yan-kee Doo-dle came to town, — Rid - ing on a po - ny;

Stuck a feath- er in his cap And called it Mac - a - ro - ni.

Refrain

Yan - kee Doo - dle keep it up, Yan - kee Doo-dle dan - dy,

Mind the mu - sic and the step And with the girls be hand - y.

2. Fath'r and I went down to camp,
Along with Captain Goodwin,
And there we saw the men and boys,
As thick as hasty pudding.

3. There was Captain Washington
Upon a slapping stallion,
A-giving orders to his men;
I guess there was a million.

A phrase is a musical thought. It is like a sentence or part of a sentence. The musical thought matches the thought in the words. We breathe at the end of a musical thought, or phrase.

The Bridge of Avignon

Are these phrases
long or short?
Which of them are alike?

WORDS BY M. V. BANNON
FRENCH FOLK TUNE

Gaily

Come and dance, as in France, For the pleas - ure

of each meas - ure, Come a - long, sing this song,

As we do in A - vi - gnon.

1. Now the boys bow this way,
   Les mes-sieurs font comm' ça,

Girls will curt - sy this way.
   et les filles font comm' ça.

2. Soldiers marching this way,
   Drummers playing this way.

Walking Song

TRADITIONAL

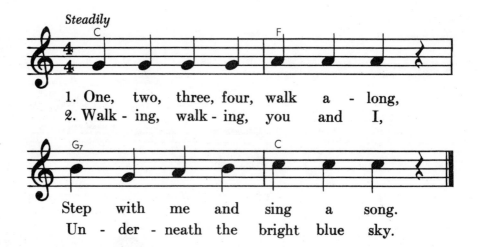

Steadily

1. One, two, three, four, walk a - long,
2. Walk - ing, walk - ing, you and I,

Step with me and sing a song.
Un - der - neath the bright blue sky.

Sing "Walking Song" and clap the basic beat.
You will see that each line ends with a quarter rest.
A rest is as important as a note.
A quarter rest has the same time value as a quarter note.

Groups of notes are divided into *measures*.
Bar lines mark off these measures.

bar line   bar line

A measure is the space between two bar lines.
The first beat of a measure is usually strong.

At the beginning of each song you will see two numbers.
This is called the *meter signature* or *time signature*.

Two common time signatures are $\frac{2}{4}$ and $\frac{4}{4}$.

$\frac{4}{4}$ can also be written **C** . You will also see **¢** .

¢ is called "cut time." There are still four quarter notes in each measure,
but the measure is divided into two beats instead of four.

94

Time signatures are written with numbers. The upper number tells you how many beats there are in a measure. The lower number tells you what kind of note gets one beat.

2/4 two beats in a measure
- ♩ quarter note gets one beat
- 𝄽 quarter rest gets one beat
- ♩ half note gets two beats
- ▬ half rest gets two beats

4/4 four beats in a measure
- ♩ quarter note gets one beat
- 𝄽 quarter rest gets one beat
- ♩ half note gets two beats
- ▬ half rest gets two beats
- o whole note gets four beats
- ▬ whole rest gets four beats

Clap or chant the following rhythms. As you clap or chant, you may want to count the beats.

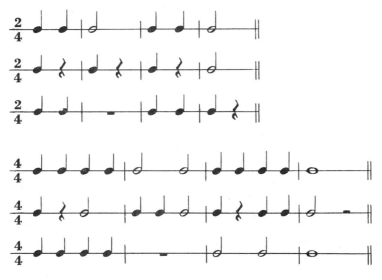

A *slur* connects notes of different pitch. Sing smoothly on one word or syllable the tones that are slurred together.

Hush, My Babe

WORDS BY ISAAC WATTS
MUSIC BY ROUSSEAU

Hush, my __ babe, lie still and slum - ber,

Ho - ly __ an - gels guard __ thy __ bed.

Read the following tunes with syllables and numbers. Then sing with "loo," connecting the tones that are slurred.

so la so mi
5   6   5   3

so mi
5   3

A *tie* connects tones of the same pitch.

Tied notes are held for the combined time value of both notes.

The half note above = 2 beats. The quarter note = 1 beat.

   2 + 1 = 3 beats. The tied notes are held 3 beats.

The dotted half note = 3 beats. The half note = 2 beats.

   3 + 2 = 5 beats. These tied notes are held 5 beats.

Read the following song, "Skater's Waltz," holding the tied notes for the proper number of beats.

Skater's Waltz

WORDS BY ROBERT REYNOLDS
MUSIC BY E. WALDTEUFEL

Here are some tunes that have common melodic patterns which you will find in many songs. Read and sing them. Look for the same patterns in other songs. This will help you to read music.

TONES SOUNDING TOGETHER

The Telephone Song

WORDS BY RENE MARTIN
CHORD MELODY

Gaily

Hel - lo!   Hel - lo!   Hel - lo!   Hel - lo!

1. We keep on say - ing, With - out de - lay - ing,
2. We're al - ways smil - ing, When we are dial - ing,
3. Your num - ber's ring - ing, While we are sing - ing,

Hel - lo!   Hel - lo!   Hel - lo!   Hel - lo!

99

Slumber Time

WORDS AND MUSIC BY NORMAN LUBOFF
ADAPTED FROM A SWEDISH LULLABY

The descant uses only three tones.
To help learn the descant, play
it on the bells as you sing.

Softly

Lull - a - by, _____ lull - a - by. __

Slum - ber time is draw-ing near, Night is gath-'ring_round us,
Stars will all be bright and clear, When the sand-man has found us.

Lull - a - by, _____ lull - a -

Dream sweet dreams the long night_ through, Moth-er will be

by, _____ lull - a - by.

near to __ you, Go to sleep, my __ dear one.

2. Pleasant dreams will come to you
   While you peacefully slumber;
   Stars will shine the long night through,
   Twinkling stars without number.
   Lulla, lulla, lullaby,
   Lulla, lulla, lullaby,
   Go to sleep, my dear one.

Hark, the Vesper Hymn is Stealing

WORDS BY THOMAS MOORE
RUSSIAN HYMN MELODY

Smoothly

Hark, the ves - per hymn is steal - ing
Near - er yet and near - er peal - ing,

O'er the wa - ters soft and clear;
Soft it breaks up - on the ear.

Joyfully

Ding - dong, ding - dong, ding - dong, ding - dong.

Ju - bi - la - te, ju - bi - la - te, Ju - bi - la - te, A - men.

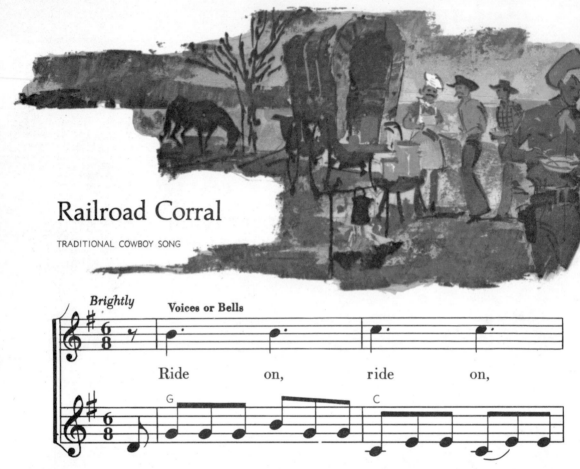

Railroad Corral

TRADITIONAL COWBOY SONG

Brightly   Voices or Bells

Ride on, ride on,

We're up in the morn-ing ere break-ing of day, __ The
The herds are a-stir o-ver hill-side and dale, With the

Fine

Ride on, ride!

chuck wag-on's bus-y, the flap-jack's in play;
night rid-ers push-ing them on-to the trail.

102

Whoop - i - ti - yi - ay, Whoop - i - ti - yi - ay!

D. C. al Fine

Swing out your raw - hides and give them full play;

Row, Row, Row Your Boat

TRADITIONAL ROUND

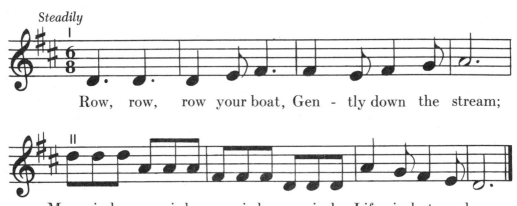

Row, row, row your boat, Gen - tly down the stream;

Mer - ri - ly, mer-ri- ly, mer-ri- ly, mer-ri - ly, Life is but a dream.

This song is a round for two groups of singers. When the first group reaches number II, the second group begins to sing at number I. Each group may sing the entire song many times, then it will go "round and round." The last time through, group one will finish four measures before group two.

Polly Wolly Doodle

TRADITIONAL

Lively

1. Oh, I went down South for to see my Sal,
2. Oh, my Sal she is a ___ maid - en fair,

Sing Pol - ly wol - ly doo - dle all the day;

My ___ Sal she is a ___ spunk - y gal,
With ___ curl - y eyes and ___ laugh - ing hair,

Sing Pol - ly wol - ly doo - dle all the day.

3. Oh, a grasshopper sittin' on a railroad track,...
   A pickin' his teeth with a carpet tack,...

4. Behind the barn, down on my knees,...
   I thought I heard a chicken sneeze,...

5. He sneezed so hard with the whoopin' cough,...
   He sneezed his head and tail right off,...

Refrain

Fare thee well,   fare thee well,   Fare -well, my fay,

Melody

Fare thee well,   fare thee well,   Fare thee well my fai - ry fay,

Pol -   ly   wol - ly ____

For I'm off to Loui- si - an - a, For to see my Su - sy - an -na,

____ doo -   dle   all   day.

Sing Pol - ly wol - ly doo - dle all the day.

When you have learned the melody, add the second
part. It uses the same notes as the melody, but the
notes have different time values. You may also play
the second part on melody bells or flute.

The cuckoo sings in April,
The cuckoo sings in May,
The cuckoo sings in June,
In July, she flies away.

The cuckoo drinks cold water
To make her sing so clear,
And then she sings "Cuckoo!"
For three months in the year.

Winter is Over

WORDS ADAPTED BY JOHN HALL
ITALIAN FOLK TUNE

Moderately

Voices or Flutes

Ooh, _____ Ooh, _____

1. The win - ter time is   o - ver, the month of A - pril gone,
2. The snow on ev -'ry moun - tain is melt - ing ver - y fast,
3. A girl stands by her win - dow, to hear the cuck - oo sing,

Ooh, _____ Ooh, _____

Now comes the month of May, when you hear the cuck - oo's song.
And now the pret - ty cuck - oo can build her nest at last.
To think a - bout her sweet - heart and wel - come in the spring.

Refrain

Cuck - oo,   cuck - oo,

Cuck - oo,   cuck - oo,

She's sing - ing all day long,

She's sing - ing all day long,
L'a - pri - le non c'è piu,

Ooh, _____ Ooh, _____ Cuck-oo.

Now comes the month of May, when you hear the cuck-oo's song. __
e rit - or - na - to è mag - gio col can - to del cu - cù. __

Birds are Sweetly Singing

WORDS BY FLORENCE MARTIN
ITALIAN FOLK MELODY

To fit the mood of the words,
sing the added part very smoothly.

Smoothly

Ah,_____ Ah,_____

1. Birds are sweet-ly sing-ing, The grass from earth is spring-ing,
2. Breez-es gen-tly blow-ing, The sun is bright-ly glow-ing,

Ah,_____ Ah._____

Now buds on stems are cling-ing, Be-cause it's spring-time.
The flow'rs and fields are grow-ing, Be-cause it's sum-mer.

3. Colored leaves are dying,
   In fields the frost is lying,
   And birds are southward flying,
   Because it's autumn.

4. Winds are cold and biting,
   The snow, the ground is bright'ning,
   Good sledding is inviting,
   Because it's winter.

Sombrero

WORDS AND MUSIC
BY WALTER WITTEL

Rhythmically

Tambourine

(Repeat throughout)

Fine

Ay,   Ay,   Ay,   Ay, *(O-lé!)*

I want a big *som - bre - ro, —* To put up - on my head; *(O-lé!)*
I want a long *se - ra - pe, —* All yel-low, green, and red. *(O-lé!)*

Ay,   Ay,

When I put them on, you see,

D. C. al Fine

Ay,   Ay.

All the folks will smile at me;

MAKING UP MUSIC

Here is a song about a clock:

Tick - tock, tick - tock, goes the lit - tle clock,

Night and day it just says "tick - tock";

O - pen wide the door of the lit - tle clock,

"Cuck - oo, cuck - oo, cuck - oo, cuck - oo."

While some sing this song, others can sing or play on bells the following tunes, repeating them over and over.

Tick - tock, tick - tock, tick - tock, tick - tock

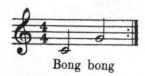

Bong bong

Cuck- oo, cuck- oo

Have you ever noticed how many different kinds of clocks there are and the different sounds they make? What kind of clock are you when you sing or play the following rhythms?

STICKS

CYMBALS

TRIANGLE

Music has a steady *beat* which we feel over and over again. Some beats are stronger than others. These are *accented* beats.

Divide into five groups and play the following rhythms. Play them first one by one and then all together.

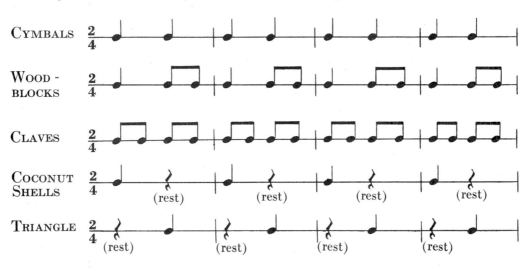

CYMBALS

WOOD-
BLOCKS

CLAVES

COCONUT
SHELLS

TRIANGLE

Perhaps one of the instruments you have is not included. Make up a rhythm for it. The more instruments, the more fun.

Rhymes and Rhythms

Poetry like music has accents and rhythm. Read the rhyme in the rhythm shown below. Someone may play the accents on a drum. Notice the measure bar comes *before each accent.*

It's rain - ing, it's   pour - ing, the   old   man is   snor - ing.

Somebody may think of a tune for these words. Here is one:

It's rain - ing, it's pour - ing, The old   man is   snor - ing.

As some sing and the drum beats out the accents, others may try to fit the following word patterns to the tune:

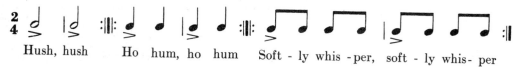

Hush, hush   Ho hum, ho hum   Soft - ly whis - per, soft - ly whis- per

Say these words in rhythm and play them on instruments as the song is sung. Then choose a tone of the following chord for each pattern and sing them one by one and together as the tune is sung.

This is the I chord:

It is fun to find the rhythm of words. Try to find the rhythm of your name by saying it over and over and beating it on the drum. Sometimes we think of a tune when we say words in rhythm. Can you find a tune for your name?

Here is a rhythmic "question" that may be clapped or may be played on instruments. Can you "answer" this "question" with a different rhythmic pattern?

Can you make up words for this "question" and "answer"? Words for the question might be "Have you a drum that goes boom, boom?" Do these rhythms and words suggest a tune?

Make up other rhythmic questions and answers, playing them on different instruments. Then think up words for them and, as you say the words, listen for a tune.

Now you are ready to play the game of musical question and answer. Everyone should take a turn at singing or playing on bells their answer to the following tune:

What is your answer? See if you can end your tune on the keynote, which is *do* or 1.

When all have had a turn at playing or singing an answer with "loo," the teacher may sing the question with words. Each of you can answer, with words put to your own tune.

Writing Music

A phrase is a musical thought. This one is unfinished.

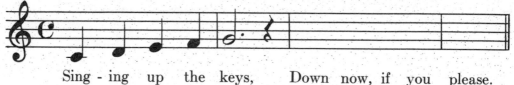

Sing - ing   up   the   keys,   Down   now,   if   you   please.

Sing the first two measures. Then try to sing to the end. The words, "Down now, if you please," tell you the direction your melody should go.

Can you write your melody in your music notebook?
One way to write music, so we can remember it, is to show the direction of the tones with lines that give an idea of their length. The tune on the staff above would look like this:

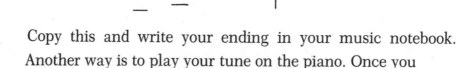

Copy this and write your ending in your music notebook.

Another way is to play your tune on the piano. Once you have found the pitches, use the chart below to write them.

1   2   3   4   5   6   7   8
do   re   mi   fa   so   la   ti   do

Complete this phrase, following the suggestion of the words.

Up a - gain we go, This time to high *do*.

When you have sung the end of this phrase, try to write it.

Now, starting on high *do*, make up a descending melody using the following words:

Sing from high to low,
To the home tone, *do*.

Write your melody in your music notebook. If you can sing a melody with syllables, you can write it without a piano.

Now you are ready to make up a song all your own. It will have two phrases. The following words suggest an ascending pattern, then a descending pattern.

See us running up the hill,
'Way up to the top.
Now we're running back again,
When we're down, we stop.

Before making up your melody, it will help if you speak the words aloud several times and listen to their rhythm. Find the accented words or parts of words. Then write the words, putting a measure bar before each accent.

See us run-ning|up the hill, |'Way up to the|top.

To find the meter signature, clap each accent. Call each accent *1* or *one*. How far can you count between accents?

115

Introductions and Codas

Complete this melody:

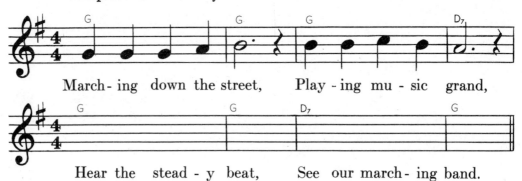

March-ing down the street, Play - ing mu - sic grand,

Hear the stead - y beat, See our march - ing band.

You may want to repeat part of the first phrase in writing a second phrase, or you may want something that is different. Make sure your melody ends in a way that sounds complete.

Can you make up additional verses about a big parade? Think of flags, soldiers, horses, floats, and gay balloons. There are many different kinds of parades.

Now that we have a song to sing about a parade, with many interesting verses to sing to it, we will want to add on an *introduction* that we can sing or play on instruments.

In order to make a really impressive parade, the marchers must all keep in step. That is why parades have bands. To introduce our song, "The Parade," we may all chant in rhythm, "One, two, three, four; one, two, three, four."

116

Or we might use a simple tune, such as

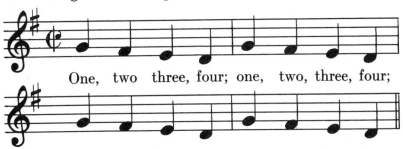

One, two three, four; one, two, three, four;

One, two, three, four; one, two, three, four.

We may use the same pattern as a *coda*, or ending.

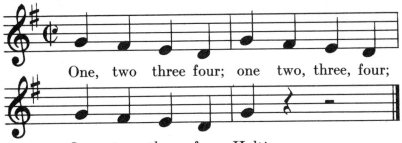

One, two three four; one two, three, four;

One, two, three, four; Halt!

There are many songs in your music book that suggest good introductions and codas. Make up simple one-measure patterns to go with songs on pages 25, 36, 75, 76, 120.

Look in your reading books for poems that suggest a tune. Short poems like the following, by Dee Harris, are good.

> Sitting on a seesaw,
>   Soaring up on high,
> Bouncing on a seesaw,
>   Riding to the sky.

Now see if you can make up a complete song, both words and music. The following titles may give you an idea for your song: "My Dog," "A Rainy Day," "Jumping Rope," "Flying Kites."

ACTING OUT SONGS

This Little Railroad Light

WORDS BY RICHARD EVANS
TRADITIONAL MELODY

Lively

1. This lit-tle rail-road light of mine,
2. Hold the — cars at the de-pot sign,

I'm going to make it shine.

This lit-tle rail-road light of mine,
Hold the — cars at the de-pot sign,

I'm going to make it shine.

On the next page are directions for signalling a train. Pretend you are holding a lantern and give the proper signals for each of the verses.

This lit-tle rail-road light of mine,
Hold the __ cars at the de-pot sign,

I'm going to make it shine, Make it

shine, make it shine, make it shine. __

3. Move them ahead, don't trail behind,
　　I'm going to make it shine,
　Move them ahead, don't trail behind,
　　I'm going to make it shine.
　Move them ahead, don't trail behind,
　　I'm going to make it shine,
　Make it shine, make it shine, make it shine.

4. Back them up on the switch-yard line,
　　I'm going to make it shine,
　Back them up on the switch-yard line,
　　I'm going to make it shine.
　Back them up on the switch-yard line,
　　I'm going to make it shine,
　Make it shine, make it shine, make it shine.

1. Hold the lantern high above your head. This means **release brakes.**
2. Hold the lantern in front of you and swing it back and forth. This means **stop.**
3. Raise and lower the lantern in front of you. This means **proceed.**
4. Swing the lantern in a circle at arm's length. This means **back up.**

She'll be Comin' 'Round the Mountain

SOUTHERN FOLK SONG

1. She'll be com-in' 'round the moun-tain when she comes, ____

She'll be com-in' round the moun-tain when she comes, ____

She'll be com-in' round the moun-tain,

She'll be com-in' round the moun-tain,

She'll be com-in' round the moun-tain when she comes. ____

2. She'll be drivin' six white horses when she comes, *(Whoa, Back!)*

3. Oh, we'll all go out to meet her when she comes, *(Hi, Babe!)*

4. Oh, we'll all have chicken and dumplings when she comes, *(Um-um!)*

120

Planting Our Garden

WORDS BY MADGE WALLIS
FRENCH FOLK TUNE

Cheerfully

1. Plant - ing our gar - den, Ver - y ear - ly in the spring-time,

We hoe the ground and pull the weeds, Then we make the rows

and plant the seeds, Ver - y ear - ly in the spring-time.

2. Tending our garden,
   Very early in the springtime,
   We water here, we water there,
   And we surely hope the weather's fair,
   Very early in the springtime.

3. Our garden's growing,
   Very early in the springtime,
   The new shoots peep up, fresh and green,
   All the lettuce, carrots, peas, and beans,
   Very early in the springtime.

Down on the Farm

A PLAYLET WITH SONGS FROM YOUR BOOK

CHARACTERS

BILL, a boy from town
BOB, his friend
UNCLE JOE, a farmer

RANDY, a boy from the country
SALLY, MARY AND MOLLY, girls
   from the country

The curtain opens on a farm scene showing barn at right.
Bob and Bill enter.

(Song: "Hiking Through the Country," p. 24)

BOB:	I'm not sure where we are but it's certainly open country.
BILL:	Look at that big red house over there.
BOB:	That's not a house, that's a barn.
BILL:	Then it's a house for animals.
BOB:	I suppose you could think of it that way. I wonder where all the people are?
BILL:	Here comes somebody now.
BOB:	Let's hide behind this tree until we see who it is.

(Enter Randy in overalls and straw hat. He sings, "The Grasshopper and the Ants," p. 70. At conclusion of song, Randy enters the barn. Bill and Bob come from behind the tree.)

BILL:	What kind of a song was that?
BOB:	It's a song with a moral.
BILL:	What's a moral?
BOB:	It's something good for you.
BILL:	Like medicine?
BOB:	Worse.

(Randy appears at barn door.)

RANDY:	Hi! What are you doing here?
BILL:	We came to see what life on a farm is like.
RANDY:	You're from town, I see. Well, I'll be glad to show you around our farm. Guess you don't get to know animals in a city.
BILL:	Yes, we do.

122

RANDY:	What kind of animals?
BILL:	Oh, raccoons, elephants, birds, and monkeys.
RANDY:	What kind of a barn do you keep them in?
BOB:	We call it a zoo.

(Bob and Bill sing, "The Animal Fair," p. 139)

RANDY:	But what good are elephants and monkeys?
BOB:	What good are all your animals?
RANDY:	Well, we get eggs from the chickens, milk from the cows, the horse pulls the plow, the donkey pulls the cart, the rooster wakes us up, and we get wool from the sheep.
BOB:	Sounds like everybody's got a job on the farm. Do you have to do most of the work?
RANDY:	Oh, no. I get a lot of help. The girls milk the cows, gather eggs, and make sure the sheep don't wander off.
BOB:	How do they do that?
RANDY:	Here come Sally, Mary, and Molly. They help one another. But Mary has her own way of herding the sheep.

(Girls enter, singing, "She Watched Her Sheep," p. 81)

SALLY:	Who are these boys?
RANDY:	They're from the city. They came out to see what farm life was like.
MARY:	They may not see much. The sky is getting awfully dark and the wind is getting stronger.
MOLLY:	We don't have to worry about that.
SALLY:	Why not?
MOLLY:	Because the wind told me nothing is going to happen.
MARY:	As though you could understand the wind.
MOLLY:	Well, I can . . . so there.

(Mary and Sally, joined by Randy, sing "Sky Music," p. 14)

MARY:	*(to Molly, who looks hurt)*. Now, Molly, don't be upset. Remember we have to work together.
BOB:	What kind of work do you do?
MARY:	Well, you know we tend the sheep, and we milk the cows sometimes, and we plant gardens.
BILL:	How do you plant a garden?
BOB:	And what do you grow?

(The girls sing, "Planting Our Garden," p. 121)

BILL:	It sounds like a lot of work.
SALLY:	It's not so bad. And it's healthy to be out of doors.
BOB:	Do you do all this yourselves?
MARY:	Most of it. If the work gets too hard we have the horse or the donkey to pull the plow for us.
MOLLY:	But we like the donkey better because the horse is awfully big.
RANDY:	Let's tell them about Aw-ee-aw and Ee-aw-ee.
BOB:	Who are they?
RANDY:	You'll see.

(The girls and Randy sing, "Two Little Donkeys," p. 136.
At conclusion of song, Uncle Joe enters.)

JOE:	Did I hear you singing about Aw-ee-aw?
RANDY:	That's right, Uncle Joe.
JOE:	Appears to me you young 'uns should be working.
SALLY:	But, Uncle Joe, the chores are all done.
JOE:	That's all right, then. The time for enjoying yourselves is after the work is done.
MARY:	Will we have a good day for our picnic, Uncle Joe?
JOE:	Oh, my yes. Nothing to worry about there.
BILL:	How can you tell?
JOE:	I can tell by the clouds.
BOB:	But how?
JOE:	It's not hard. There are sad clouds and happy clouds. When the clouds are sad they cry, just like we do, but when the clouds are happy they let the sun shine and we have a bright day.

(Uncle Joe sings, "Clouds," p. 37)

SALLY:	Uncle Joe can tell all sorts of things.
MOLLY:	He can tell where the fish are in the water.
MARY:	And where the best berries grow.
RANDY:	And when it's the best time to plant.
BOB:	Can you tell when the snow will come?
BILL:	Or when is the best time to plow a field?
JOE:	Now, children, one question at a time.

(All sing, "Hop Up, My Ladies," p. 26. Uncle Joe joins in
the chorus and they conclude with a dance.)

CURTAIN

Sheep Shearing Song

Pretend you are doing all the things mentioned in the song.

WORDS BY FLORENCE MARTIN
NORWEGIAN FOLK TUNE

1. Come, let __ us __ shear the __ sheep, Shear them well! __ Work and __ sing!
2. Come, let __ us __ card the __ wool, Card it __ well! __ Work and __ sing!

Come let __ us __ shear the __ sheep, Then we'll __ go __ danc- ing!
We shall __ knit __ stock-ings __ fine, Then we'll __ go __ danc- ing!

Refrain

Press, press the trea - dle and keep the __ wheel spin - ning!

Fin - ish the weav - ing, so we can __ go __ danc-ing!

3. Come, let us dye the yarn,
   Dye it well! Work and sing!
   We shall knit sweaters fine,
   Then we'll go dancing!

4. Come, let us weave the cloth,
   Weave it well! Work and sing!
   We shall make clothing fine,
   Then we'll go dancing!

125

Three Pirates

ENGLISH FOLK SONG

Before you sing this
song, read the words in
the rhythm of the melody.
Pretend you are jolly
pirates as you sing.

Brightly

1. Three pi - rates came to Lon - don town,⎫ Yo ho, Yo ho,
2. At first they came to a way - side inn,⎭

Three pi - rates came to Lon - don town,⎫ Yo ho, Yo ho,
At first they came to a way - side inn,⎭

Three pi - rates came to Lon - don town, To
At first they came to a way - side inn, And

see the king put on his crown,⎫ Yo ho, you lub - bers, Yo
said, "Good land - lord, let us in;"⎭

ho, you lub - bers, Yo ho, Yo ho, Yo ho!

126

3. "O landlord, have you hoards of gold,
   Yo ho, Yo ho,
   O landlord, have you hoards of gold,
   Yo ho, Yo ho,
   O landlord, have you hoards of gold,
   Enough to fill the afterhold?"

4. "Oh, yes sir, I have hoards of gold,
   Enough to fill the afterhold."

5. "O landlord, have you a daughter fair,
   With laughing eyes and curly hair?"

6. "Oh, yes sir, I've a daughter fair,
   With laughing eyes and curly hair."

7. "O landlord, will she marry me,
   And sail with me across the sea?"

8. "Oh, yes sir, she will marry thee,
   And sail with thee across the sea."

Alouette

FRENCH-CANADIAN FOLK SONG

Brightly

Chorus

A - lou - et - te, gen - tille A - lou - et - te,
A - lou - et - te, Je te plu - me - rai.

Solo

1. Je te plu - me - rai la tête,
2. Je te plu - me - rai le bec,

Chorus

Je te plu - me - rai la tête,
Je te plu - me - rai le bec,

Verses accumulate

Et la tête, Et la tête,
Et le bec, Et le bec, } Oh!

3. *le nez* (nose)   4. *le dos* (back)   5. *les pieds* (feet)

Haul on the Line, Boys

TRADITIONAL SEA CHANTEY

Steadily

Voices or Bells

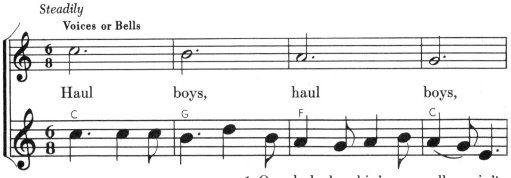

Haul   boys,   haul   boys,

C   G   F   C

1. Our bul-ly ship's a-roll-in'!
Haul   on the line, boys,   2. Our cap-tain, he's a-growl-in'!
3. Oh, Dai-sy, you're my dar-lin'!

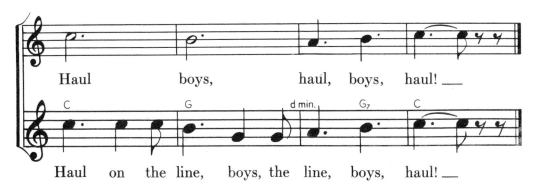

Haul   boys,   haul, boys, haul! __

C   G   d min.   G₇   C

Haul   on   the line,   boys, the line,   boys,   haul! __

129

Malbrough

WORDS BY RENE MARTIN
FRENCH FOLK TUNE

The class may enjoy
acting out the story of
this old song about the
famous General Malbrough.

1. Mal - brough to war is go - ing, With his
2. We hear the bu - gles blow - ing, Ta - ta -

sword and lance he is go - ing, Mal-brough to war is
ta, the bu - gles are blow - ing, We hear the bu - gles

go - ing, We'll sing till he gets back.____
blow - ing, We'll sing till they get back.____

We'll sing till he gets back,__ We'll sing till he gets back, __
We'll sing till they get back,__ We'll sing till they get back, __

3. We hear the field drums rumbling,
   Pum-pum-pum, the field drums
      are rumbling,
   We hear the field drums rumbling,
   We'll sing till they get back.

4. Malbrough is now returning,
   With his sword and lance
      he's returning,
   Malbrough is now returning,
   Our singing brought him back.

130

FUN AND NONSENSE

The Old Gray Goose

TRADITIONAL

Cheerfully

Look - a right here and look - a right there, Look 'way

o - ver yon - der; Don't you see the old gray goose

A - smil - in' at the gan - der, A - smil - in',

a - smil - in', A - smil - in' at the gan - der?

I Can't Spell Hippopotamus

WORDS AND MUSIC
BY J. FRED COOTS

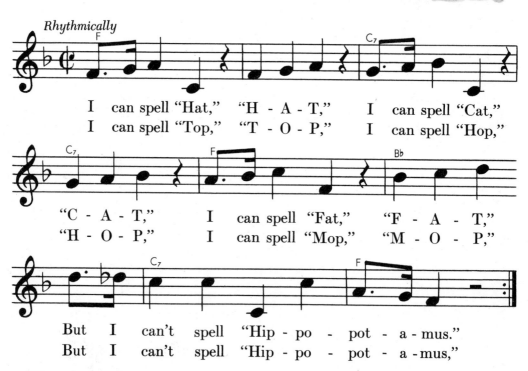

Rhythmically

I can spell "Hat," "H - A - T," I can spell "Cat,"
I can spell "Top," "T - O - P," I can spell "Hop,"

"C - A - T," I can spell "Fat," "F - A - T,"
"H - O - P," I can spell "Mop," "M - O - P,"

But I can't spell "Hip - po - pot - a - mus."
But I can't spell "Hip - po - pot - a - mus,"

132

"H - I - P - P - O" I know, And then comes

"P - O - T," But that's as far as

I can go, And that's what both-ers me, Gee!

I can spell "Dog," "D - O - G," I can spell "Log,"

"L - O - G," I can spell "Hog," "H - O - G,"

But I can't spell "Hip - po - pot - a - mus."

You may enjoy making up other verses to sing. Use only three letter words that rhyme. To start, you might use "ban," "man," and "fan." Now try "tag."

Riqui Ran

WORDS ADAPTED BY ADELE LEONARD
LATIN AMERICAN FOLK SONG

Pan is bread,
alfenique is sugar paste,
and **alfondoque** is brown sugar.

Brightly

1. Ri - qui, ri - qui, ri - qui ran, All the woods-men
2. Ri - qui, ri - qui, ri - qui ran, Where have all the

of San Juan Eat their cheese and eat their *pan.* Those from
chil- dren gone? They have put their night-gowns on. They will

Ri - que, *al - fe - ni - que;* Those from Ro - que, *al - fon -*
dream of *al - fe - ni - que;* And, to - mor- row, *al - fon -*

do - que; Ri - qui, ri - qui, ri - qui ran, Ri - qui,
do - que; Ri - qui, ri - qui, ri - qui ran, Ri - qui,

ri - qui, ri - qui ran, All the woods -men of San Juan.
ri - qui, ri - qui ran, Where have all the chil-dren gone?

134

Map Reading Song

1. Reading maps is fun for me,
   All I need is one small key,
   With it I know where to go.
   When I see a blue line
      showing,
   I can tell there's water
      flowing;
   And I know that two red
      lines
   Show me where a highway
      winds.
   Let's explore some other signs.

2. When I see a big black dot,
   There's a town right near
      that spot.
   Roads are straight black lines,
      you know.
   Railroads look like someone's
      sewing,
   Green's for parks where grass
      is growing.
   All the symbols that you see
   Can be fun, you will agree,
   When you use a little key!

The above words, by Madeleine A. Dufay, were written to be sung to the tune of "Riqui Ran."

Chumbara

CANADIAN SCHOOL SONG

Gaily

1. Chum - ba - ra, ____ chum - ba - ra, chum - ba - ra, ____
2. Fy - do - lee, ____ fy - do - lee, fy - do - lee, ____

chum - ba - ra, chum - ba - ra, ____ chum - ba - ra,
fy - do - lee, fy - do - lee, ____ fy - do - lee,

1.
chum chum chum chum chum chum chum chum chum chum!
fy fy fy fy fy fy fy fy fy fy!

2.
Shout
Hi!

Two Little Donkeys

WORDS AND MUSIC
BY VIC MARANTZ

Cheerfully

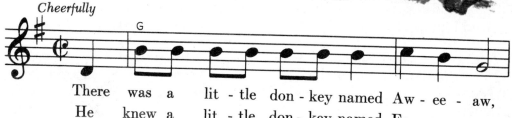

There was a lit - tle don - key named Aw - ee - aw,
He knew a lit - tle don - key named Ee - aw - ee,

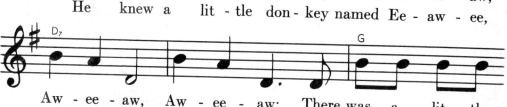

Aw - ee - aw, Aw - ee - aw; There was a lit - tle
Ee - aw - ee, Ee - aw - ee, He knew a lit - tle

don - key named Aw - ee - aw, Trot, trot, trot-ty wot home.
don - key named Ee - aw - ee, Trot, trot, trot- ty wot home.

Now Aw - ee - aw and Ee - aw - ee, They were the

ver - y best friends, you see; Well, _____ They

136

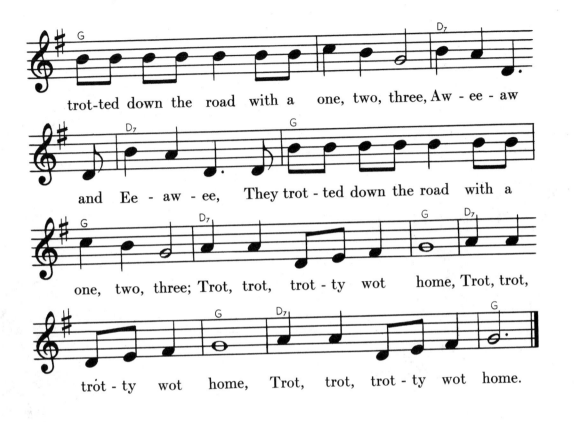

trot-ted down the road with a one, two, three, Aw - ee - aw

and Ee - aw - ee, They trot - ted down the road with a

one, two, three; Trot, trot, trot - ty wot home, Trot, trot,

trot - ty wot home, Trot, trot, trot - ty wot home.

On the Trail

FROM "GRAND CANYON SUITE"
BY FERDE GROFE

This piece is a musical trip down the Grand Canyon. In it you will hear a waterfall, a stream, and the hee-haws of the burros.

This melody sounds like the clip-clop of the burros' hooves.

What do you hear at the end of the piece?

The Bird and the Frog

WORDS BY CLAUDIA REGEN
GERMAN FOLK TUNE

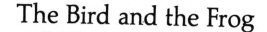

Gaily

1. In a tree a bird was sing - ing, You could
2. In a pond a frog was soak - ing, You could
3. Said the frog,"Let's sing to - geth - er," Said the

hear her sweet voice ring- ing, Twee twee, chee chee,
hear his mer - ry croak- ing, Grok grok, brp brp,
bird,"I'm will - ing to, sir," { Twee twee, chee chee,
{ Grok grok, brp brp,

Twee twee twee tweet-y tweet - y twee, Chee chee chee chee chee,
Grok grok grok grok-y grok - y grok, Brp brp brp brp brp,
Twee twee twee tweet-y tweet- y twee. } Don't you all a - gree,
Grok grok grok grok-y grok - y grok.

Girls may sing the part of the bird in verse 1. And boys the frog in verse 2. Each group sings his own words in verse 3.

twee twee, twee, twee twee;   Up and down the notes were trill- ing.
grok grok grok grok grok; Said the bird, "You must be   jok - ing."
sing - ing sep-'rate - ly   For a frog and bird is   bet - ter?

The Animal Fair

TRADITIONAL

Cheerfully

(Continue throughout)

The monk, the   monk, the   monk, the monk

I   went to   the an - i - mal fair, — The birds and the beasts were
The fun - ni - est was — the monk, — He climbed up the el-e-phant's

there, — The old   ra - coon, by the   light   of   the moon, Was
trunk, —

comb - ing   her   au - burn hair. — The   el - e - phant sneezed

and   fell   on   his knees, And what   be - came   of   the monk? —

How Many?

WORDS AND MUSIC
BY ALFRED STERN

How many repeated notes
can you find in this song? How many ties?

Liltingly

1. How man - y rain - drops fall down from the clouds?
2. If I have one ap - ple, two ap - ples, three,

Al - most a mil - lion or two, _____
How man - y ap - ples have I? _____

How man - y stars do you see in the sky?
If I eat one ap - ple, two ap - ples, three,

May - be a bil - lion or few. _____
How man - y left for a pie? _____

How man - y birds are there fly - ing a - round?
If I throw one of them up in the air,

How man - y   fish   in   the   sea? _____
How man - y   left   in   my   hand? _____

Well, count them, count them, count them   now. __

Rhythm Round

Clap or play these patterns on your rhythm instruments:

Now play the four patterns, one after the other, without stopping.

Divide into two groups. Group 2 can wait until Group 1 reaches the end of the first line before beginning to play. Play through several times. Group 1 will finish two measures before Group 2.

Does this rhythm round remind you of a familiar song?

The song is in this book.

When you have guessed it, sing the song as a round, too.

Crocodile Song

TRADITIONAL

Happily

She sailed a - way on a bright and sun - ny day,

On the back of a croc - o - dile. "You see," said she,

"He's as tame as he can be As I float him

down the Nile." The Croc winked his eye as she

waved a mer - ry bye, Wear - ing a hap - py smile.

At the end of the ride, the la-dy was in-side,

And the smile was on the croc-o-dile. (*Clap Clap*)

Counting Song

You can learn many Spanish
words in this song.

WORDS BY LUCILLE WOOD
MEXICAN FOLK TUNE

Moderately

1. U - no, dos y tres, ___ Cua - tro, cin - co, seis,
2. Ten - go un som - bre - ro, I have a lit - tle hat,
3. A - di - os, a - mi - go, A - di - os, my friend.

Sei - te, o - cho, nue - ve, I can count to *diez.*
Ten - go un se - ra - pe, What do you think of that?
Has - ta la vis - ta. Till we meet a - gain.

In the first verse of this song, you can learn to count to ten in Spanish. The Spanish
words in the second verse mean "I have a hat," and "I have a cape." The third verse
means "Goodbye, my friend, until we meet again." You are likely to find these words
in other Spanish or Mexican songs.

Used by permission of Bowmar Records.

143

The Crawdad Hole

SOUTHERN MOUNTAIN SONG

A crawdad looks very much
like a small lobster.

Lively

1. You get a line and I'll bring a pole, Hon-ey; ___
2. What you gon-na do when the pond goes ___ dry, Hon-ey? ___

You get a line and I'll bring a pole, Ba - by. ___
What you gon-na do when the pond goes ___ dry, Ba - by? ___

You get a line and I'll bring a pole, We'll go
What you gon-na do when the pond goes ___ dry? Sit on the

fish - in' in a craw-dad hole, Hon-ey, Ba-by o' mine. ___
bank and catch an old horse-fly. Hon-ey, Ba-by o' mine. ___

3. Crawdad, crawdad, a-feelin' fine, Honey;
Crawdad, crawdad, a-feelin' fine, Baby;
Crawdad, crawdad, a-feelin' fine,
Two for a nickel and three for a dime,
Honey, Baby o' mine.

Angelico

Can you make up other verses telling
about different jobs Angelico might do?

WORDS BY HOLSAERT-BAILEY
HAITIAN MELODY

Rhythmically

An - gel - i - co, __ An - gel - i - co, __ go home to __ ma - ma;

An - gel - i - co, __ An - gel - i - co, __ go home to __ ma - ma.

1. Lit - tle girl who wash - es all the clothes, __
2. Lit - tle girl who sweeps and sweeps the floor, __

go home to __ ma - ma. She scrubs off all the
go home to __ ma - ma. She sweeps the dust right

D. C. al Fine

pret - ty bows. __ Go home to __ ma - ma.
out the door. __ Go home to __ ma - ma.

From the collection, "Sing a Song with Charity Bailey,"
© Plymouth Music Co.

Don't Take My Hoss Away

WORDS AND MUSIC
BY MABEL H. TODD

Hang me by my boots, Hang me by my head,

Take my shoot-in' iron in-stead, But don't take my

hoss a - way. _____ Take a - way my spurs,

Take a - way my gal, Life's no good with-out my pal,

So don't take my hoss a - way. _____ We

ate to - geth - er and we slept to - geth - er,

And we roamed the fields both far and near,

Shared our mis-er-y, made some his-to-ry,

My old nag's a dear, So! Hang me by my boots,

Hang me by my head, Take my shoot-in'

iron in-stead, But don't take my hoss a-way. ____

He was a Sailor

WORDS BY MADELEINE A. DUFAY
FRENCH FOLK TUNE

Lively

1. He was a sail - or dressed in blue, ___ He was a
2. He said a sail - or leaves the shore, ___ He said a

sail - or dressed in blue, ___ But he had ne - ne - nev - er
sail - or leaves the shore, ___ And sails the mi - mi - might - y

seen a boat; No, he had ne - ne - nev - er seen a
o - cean bold, And sails the mi - mi - might - y o - cean

boat, Nor been a - float! Is not for me!
bold, So I've been told!

After Verse 4 only

3. "I'll build a raft so strong and sturdy,
   And at the daw—daw—dawning of the day, I'll sail away!"

4. But when he saw the waves in motion,
   He said, "The ro—ro—rolling of the sea, Is not for me!"

SONGS FOR SPECIAL DAYS

Flag Song

WORDS AND MUSIC
BY VIRGINIA PAVELKO

Moderately

1. I stand up to sa - lute the flag,
2. Dear Lord, please bless A - mer - i - ca

My hand is on my heart,
And help my friends and me

I know the love in - side must be
to do our ver - y best to keep

The most im - por - tant part.
Our coun - try clean and free.

Trick or Treat

WORDS BY H. G. TREBILCOX
SWEDISH FOLK TUNE

Steadily

Witch - es and gob - lins, fair - ies and princ - es,
Mon - sters and hor - rors, pi - rates and gyp - sies,

1.
2.

All knock-ing at the door, }
E - ven a di - no-saur, } Trick or Treat! Trick or Treat!

On this Oc - to - ber night, Trick or Treat!

Strange crea - tures come to light, Trick or Treat!

Cow - boys and mon - keys, li - ons and ti - gers,

All call- ing, "Trick or Treat!"

For the Beauty of the Earth

WORDS BY F. S. PIERPONT
MUSIC BY CONRAD KOCHER

Moderately

1. For the ‿ beau - ty of the earth, For the beau - ty
2. For the ‿ beau - ty of each hour, Of the day and

of the skies, For the ‿ love which from our birth
of the night, Hill and ‿ vale and tree and flow'r,

O - ver and a - round us lies, ⎫
Sun and moon and stars of light, ⎬ Lord of all, to

Thee we raise This our hymn of grate - ful praise.

Hanukah

WORDS BY A. S. KNUTH
HEBREW MELODY

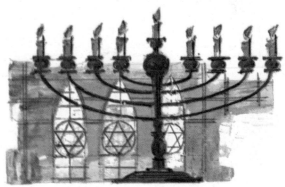

Joyfully

Ha - nu - kah, Ha - nu - kah, Dance a - round the ring,

Friends you know, smil - ing so, Ev - 'ry - bo - dy sing;

Ha - nu - kah, Ha - nu - kah, Eight nights in a row,

Dance a - long, sing a song, Hap - py hol - i - day!

Dreydl Mine

WORDS ADAPTED
HEBREW MELODY

Happily

Drey - dl mine, spin, spin, spin, Ha - nu - kah, _____
S'e - vi - von, sov, sov, sov, Ha - nu - kah, _____

Let's be - gin; Ha - nu - kah, Who will win?
Hu hag tov, Ha - nu - kah, Hu hag tov,

Lit - tle drey - dl, spin, spin, spin.
S'e - vi - von, _____ sov, sov, sov.

A dreydl is a toy which spins like a top.
Sometimes it is called **s'evivon.**

Shepherds Watched

FOLK CAROL OF THE ARABS
COLLECTED BY ROLLA FOLEY

Allegro

1. Shep - herds watched ___ their flocks in fright,
2. Prince of Peace ___ is born this night,

Star of won - der lit the night; But an an - gel
Fol - low star in sky so bright; Find the Babe ___ in

came to tell, Great - est joy that star did ___ spell.
man - ger stall, Has - ten to the Boy so ___ small.

3. Fast asleep the Christ Child lay,
   As the shepherds made their way.
   Gentle Mary, mother mild,
   Watched beside her Holy Child.

4. Joseph crooned a lullaby,
   Lest his Lad awake and cry.
   "Sleep my little one in the hay,
   God we thank for Thee this day."

154

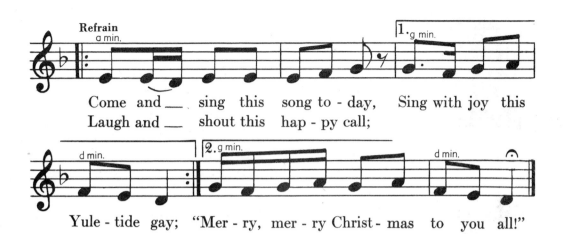

Refrain
a min.

Come and __ sing this song to - day, Sing with joy this
Laugh and __ shout this hap - py call;

d min.

Yule - tide gay; "Mer - ry, mer - ry Christ - mas to you all!"

Joseph Dearest, Joseph Mild

OLD GERMAN CAROL

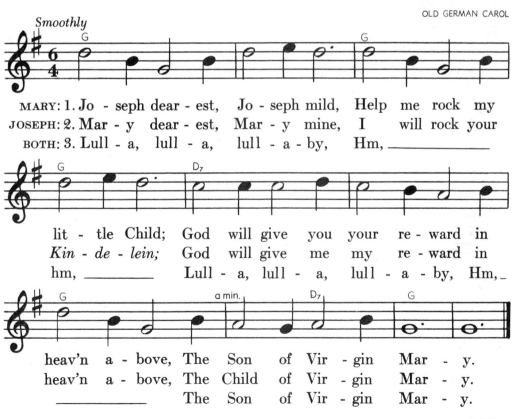

Smoothly

MARY: 1. Jo - seph dear - est, Jo - seph mild, Help me rock my
JOSEPH: 2. Mar - y dear - est, Mar - y mine, I will rock your
BOTH: 3. Lull - a, lull - a, lull - a - by, Hm, _____

lit - tle Child; God will give you your re - ward in
Kin - de - lein; God will give me my re - ward in
hm, _____ Lull - a, lull - a, lull - a - by, Hm,_

heav'n a - bove, The Son of Vir - gin Mar - y.
heav'n a - bove, The Child of Vir - gin Mar - y.
_____ The Son of Vir - gin Mar - y.

O Christmas Tree

GERMAN CAROL

O Christ-mas tree, O Christ-mas tree,

I love your spread-ing branch-es.

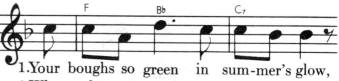

1. Your boughs so green in sum-mer's glow,
2. When oth-er trees are cold and bare,

Will nev-er fade in win-ter's snow.
At Christ-mas time, you're green and fair.

O Christ-mas tree, O Christ-mas tree,

I love your spread-ing branch-es.

My Christmas Stocking

WORDS BY MADELEINE A. DUFAY
FRENCH FOLK TUNE

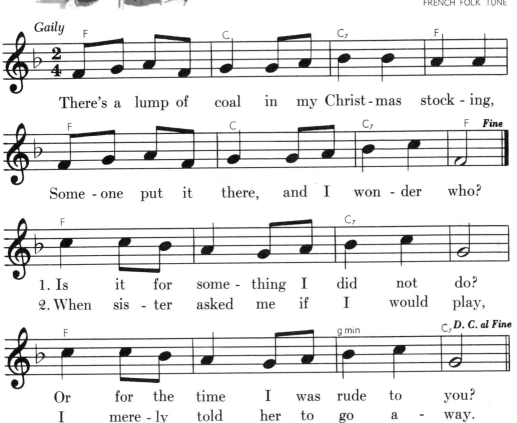

There's a lump of coal in my Christ-mas stock-ing,

Some - one put it there, and I won - der who?

1. Is it for some - thing I did not do?
2. When sis - ter asked me if I would play,

Or for the time I was rude to you?
I mere - ly told her to go a - way.

3. There's a lump of coal in my Christmas stocking,
   Guess ol' Santa knows why I got it, too.
   One day my candy I wouldn't share,
   And said a word that I shouldn't dare.

157

O Little Town of Bethlehem

WORDS BY PHILLIPS BROOKS
MUSIC BY LEWIS H. REDNER

1. O lit - tle town of Beth - le - hem, How still we __ see thee lie; A - bove thy deep and dream - less sleep The si - lent __ stars go by: Yet in thy dark streets shin - eth The ev - er - last - ing Light; The hopes and fears of all the years Are met in thee to - night.

2. For Christ is born of Mary;
   And gathered all above,
   While mortals sleep, the
     angels keep
   Their watch of wond'ring love.
   O morning stars, together
   Proclaim the holy birth;
   And praises sing to God,
     the King,
   And peace to men on earth.

He is Born

WORDS BY ADELE ST. ETIENNE
FRENCH CAROL

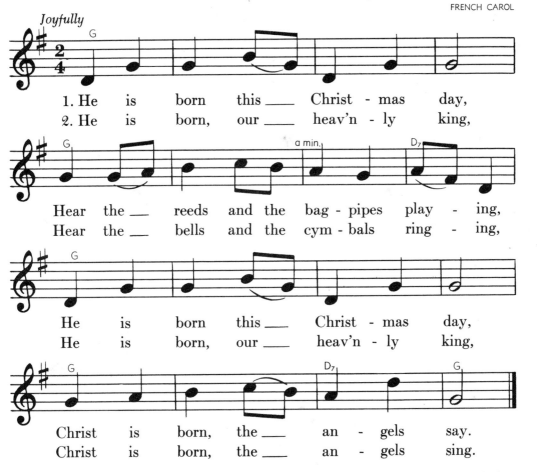

Joyfully

1. He is born this __ Christ - mas day,
2. He is born, our __ heav'n - ly king,

Hear the __ reeds and the bag - pipes play - ing,
Hear the __ bells and the cym - bals ring - ing,

He is born this __ Christ - mas day,
He is born, our __ heav'n - ly king,

Christ is born, the __ an - gels say.
Christ is born, the __ an - gels sing.

159

Frosty, the Snowman

WORDS AND MUSIC
BY STEVEN NELSON
AND JACK ROLLINS

Brightly

Frost - y, the Snow-man, was a jol - ly hap - py soul, __
Frost - y, the Snow-man, is a fair - y tale, they say, __

With a corn - cob pipe and a but - ton nose __ and two
He was made of snow, but the chil - dren know __ how he

eyes made out of coal. came to life one day.

There must have been some mag - ic in that old silk hat they

found, For when they placed it on his head, he be -

160

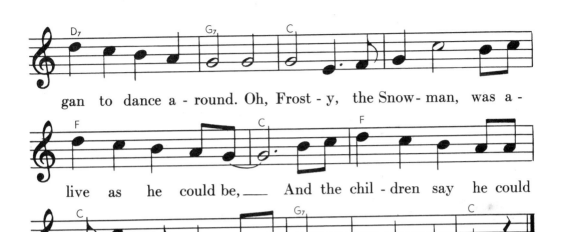

gan to dance a - round. Oh, Frost - y, the Snow - man, was a -

live as he could be, ___ And the chil - dren say he could

laugh and play ___ just the same as you and me.

Valentine Game

WORDS AND MUSIC
BY JOAN HAINES

Cheerfully

Val - en - tine! Val - en - tine! I'll be yours if

you'll be mine. Here I bring a heart that's true,

Please love me for I love you.

From "The Singing Year."
Used by permission of Clarke-Irwin and Co., Ltd.

161

There are Many Flags

WORDS BY M. H. HOWLISTON

1. There are man - y flags in man - y lands, There are
2. We shall al - ways love the stars and stripes, And we

flags of ev - 'ry hue; But there is no flag, how -
ev - er shall be true To this land of ours and the

ev - er grand, Like our own Red, White,— and— Blue.
dear old flag, Just our own Red, White,— and— Blue.

Refrain

Then hur - rah for the flag, our coun - try's flag, Its

stripes and white stars, too; For there is no flag in

an - y land Like our own Red, White,— and— Blue.

Lovely New Year Flower

WORDS BY MADU LEE
CHINESE FOLK TUNE

Peacefully

This love - ly flow - er ___ nod - ding here,

Brings joy - ous wish - es ___ for the year:

Say - ing, "Be well, in con - tent - ment dwell,

Fill all your days with ___ peace and cheer."

We think of lilies at Easter and poinsettias at Christmas.
The narcissus is the traditional Chinese New Year flower.
This holiday is celebrated either in late January or early
February. It is a very joyous occasion for everyone.

Oh, Hear the Bells Ring

WORDS ADAPTED BY CLAUDIA REGEN
GERMAN FOLK TUNE

Joyfully

1. Oh, hear the bells ring, Al - le - lu - ia they sing. The
2. Oh, hear the bells ring, Al - le - lu - ia they sing. In

joy - ful notes, with— one ac - cord, Ring out in praise of our
stir-ring tones their— voic- es say, "Pro - claim your love on this

ris - en Lord. Oh, hear the bells ring, Al - le - lu - ia they sing.
ho - ly day." Oh, hear the bells ring, Al - le - lu - ia they sing.

Easter

WORDS BY INEZ HOGAN
MUSIC BY HOAGY CARMICHAEL

Joyfully

Eas - ter - time means spring is here, Leaves and
That is why on Eas - ter Day, Chil - dren

grass and buds ap - pear; Birds will weave green
find bright eggs and say, "Spring is here, just

1. grass and make bas - kets that the bun - nies take.

2. look and see What the bun - ny left for me!"

The Dogwood Tree

WORDS BY MADELEINE A. DUFAY
GERMAN FOLK TUNE

Smoothly

1. When birds come home in ear - ly spring

and win - ter's snow is ___ done,

The dog - wood tree is reach - ing

to touch the warm - ing sun.

2. While nature tries in early spring
The sleeping earth to arouse,
The dogwood tree is showing
White blossoms on her boughs.

In the Good Old Summertime

WORDS BY REN SHIELDS
MUSIC BY GEORGE EVANS

Liltingly

Any two instruments or groups may play this pattern throughout:

In the good old sum - mer - time, ___ In the good old

sum - mer - time; ___ Stroll - ing through the shad - y lanes,

With your ba - by mine. ___ You hold her hand and she holds

yours, And that's a ver - y good sign ___ That she's your

toot - sey woot - sey In the good old sum - mer- time. ___

How many ties and dotted notes can you find in this song?

Our Pledge to America

WORDS BY JOHN HALL
MUSIC BY W. W. SCHMIDT

Moderately

A - mer - i - ca, A - mer - i - ca,

We pledge our hearts so true;

And proud - ly give al - le - giance

To our own Red, White, and Blue.

Betsy Ross, who lived in Philadelphia, is thought to have made the first United States flag, using a pattern brought to her by a committee headed by George Washington. Our flag has been given different popular names: "Red, White, and Blue," "Old Glory," and "The Stars and Stripes."

Classified Index

169

170

Song Titles

Listening Themes

Recordings and wall charts of all listening themes in *Growing with Music* are available in the Bowmar Orchestral Library.